Pray the Rosary
with
Saint John Paul II

Edited by Scott L. Smith

Pray the Rosary with Saint John Paul II
Copyright © 2019 Scott L. Smith

ISBN-13: 978-1-950782-08-6
Holy Water Books (Publisher)

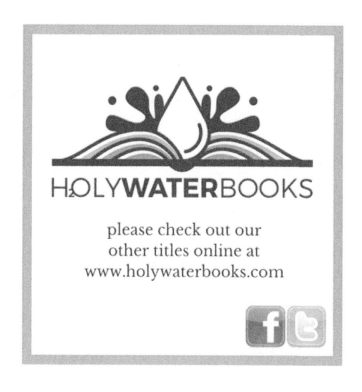

HOLYWATERBOOKS

please check out our
other titles online at
www.holywaterbooks.com

TOTUS TUUS!

Table of Contents

PART ONE:
St. John Paul II's Instructions for Praying the Rosary

From the Apostolic Letter of Saint John Paul II entitled Rosarium Virginis Mariae ("The Rosary of the Virgin Mary"):

The Rosary, a way of assimilating the mystery

Meditation on the mysteries of Christ is proposed in the Rosary by means of a method designed to assist in their assimilation. It is a method *based on repetition*. This applies above all to the *Hail Mary*, repeated ten times in each mystery. If this repetition is considered superficially, there could be a temptation to see the Rosary as a dry and boring exercise. It is quite another thing, however, when the Rosary is thought of as an outpouring of that love which tirelessly returns to the person loved with expressions similar in their content but ever fresh in terms of the feeling pervading them.

In Christ, God has truly assumed a "heart of flesh". Not only does God have a divine heart, rich in mercy and in forgiveness, but also a human heart, capable of all the stirrings of affection. If we needed evidence for this from the Gospel, we could easily find it in the touching dialogue between Christ and Peter after the Resurrection: "Simon, son of John, do you love me?" Three times this question is put to Peter, and three times he gives the reply: "Lord, you know that I love you."[1] Over and above the specific meaning of this passage, so important for Peter's mission, none can fail to recognize the beauty of this triple repetition, in which the insistent request and the corresponding reply are expressed in terms familiar from the universal experience of human love. To understand the Rosary, one has to enter into the psychological dynamic proper to love.

One thing is clear: although the repeated *Hail Mary* is addressed directly to Mary, it is to Jesus that the act of love is ultimately directed, with her and through her. The repetition is nourished by the desire to be conformed ever more completely to Christ, the true programme of the Christian life. Saint Paul expressed this project with words of fire: "For me to live is Christ and to die is gain."[2] And again: "It is no longer I that live, but Christ lives in me."[3] The Rosary

---

[1] cf. John 21:15-17
[2] Philippians 1:21
[3] Galatians 2:20

helps us to be conformed ever more closely to Christ until we attain true holiness.

A valid method...

We should not be surprised that our relationship with Christ makes use of a method. God communicates himself to us respecting our human nature and its vital rhythms. Hence, while Christian spirituality is familiar with the most sublime forms of mystical silence in which images, words and gestures are all, so to speak, superseded by an intense and ineffable union with God, it normally engages the whole person in all his complex psychological, physical and relational reality.

This becomes apparent in the Liturgy. Sacraments and sacramentals are structured as a series of rites which bring into play all the dimensions of the person. The same applies to non-liturgical prayer. This is confirmed by the fact that, in the East, the most characteristic prayer of Christological meditation, centered on the words "Lord Jesus Christ, Son of God, have mercy on me, a sinner"[4] is traditionally linked to the rhythm of breathing; while this practice favors perseverance in the prayer, it also in some way embodies the desire for Christ to become the breath, the soul and the "all" of one's life.

---

[4] Catechism of the Catholic Church, 2616.

... *which can nevertheless be improved*

I mentioned in my Apostolic Letter *Novo Millennio Ineunte* that the West is now experiencing a renewed demand for meditation, which at times leads to a keen interest in aspects of other religions.[5] Some Christians, limited in their knowledge of the Christian contemplative tradition, are attracted by those forms of prayer. While the latter contain many elements which are positive and at times compatible with Christian experience, they are often based on ultimately unacceptable premises. Much in vogue among these approaches are methods aimed at attaining a high level of spiritual concentration by using techniques of a psychophysical, repetitive and symbolic nature. The Rosary is situated within this broad gamut of religious phenomena, but it is distinguished by characteristics of its own which correspond to specifically Christian requirements.

In effect, the Rosary is simply a method of contemplation. As a method, it serves as a means to an end and cannot become an end in itself. All the same, as the fruit of centuries of experience, this method should not be undervalued. In its favor one could cite the experience of countless Saints. This is not to say, however, that the method cannot be improved. Such is the intent of the addition of the new series of *mysteria lucis* to the overall cycle of mysteries and of the few suggestions which I am proposing in this Letter regarding its manner of recitation. These suggestions, while respecting the well-established structure of this prayer, are intended to help the faithful to under-

---

[5] cf. No. 33: AAS 93 (2001), 289.

stand it in the richness of its symbolism and in harmony with the demands of daily life. Otherwise there is a risk that the Rosary would not only fail to produce the intended spiritual effects, but even that the beads, with which it is usually said, could come to be regarded as some kind of amulet or magic object, thereby radically distorting their meaning and function.

Announcing each mystery

Announcing each mystery, and perhaps even using a suitable icon to portray it, is as it were to open up a scenario on which to focus our attention. The words direct the imagination and the mind towards a particular episode or moment in the life of Christ. In the Church's traditional spirituality, the veneration of icons and the many devotions appealing to the senses, as well as the method of prayer proposed by Saint Ignatius of Loyola in the *Spiritual Exercises*, make use of visual and imaginative elements (the *compositio loci*), judged to be of great help in concentrating the mind on the particular mystery.

This is a methodology, moreover, which *corresponds to the inner logic of the Incarnation*: in Jesus, God wanted to take on human features. It is through his bodily reality that we are led into contact with the mystery of his divinity.

This need for concreteness finds further expression in the announcement of the various mysteries of the Rosary. Obviously these mysteries neither replace the Gospel nor exhaust its content. The Rosary, therefore, is no substitute for *lectio divina*; on the contrary, it presupposes and promotes it. Yet, even though the mysteries contemplated in the Rosary, even with the addition of the mysteria lucis, do no more than outline the fundamental elements of the life of Christ, they easily draw the mind to a more expansive reflection on the rest of the Gospel, especially when the Rosary is prayed in a setting of prolonged recollection.

Listening to the word of God

In order to supply a Biblical foundation and greater depth to our meditation, it is helpful to follow the announcement of the mystery with *the proclamation of a related Biblical passage*, long or short, depending on the circumstances. No other words can ever match the efficacy of the inspired word. As we listen, we are certain that this is the word of God, spoken for today and spoken "for me".

If received in this way, the word of God can become part of the Rosary's methodology of repetition without giving rise to the ennui derived from the simple recollection of something already well known. It is not a matter of recalling information but of allowing

God to speak. In certain solemn communal celebrations, this word can be appropriately illustrated by a brief commentary.

Silence

Listening and meditation are nourished by silence. After the announcement of the mystery and the proclamation of the word, it is fitting to pause and focus one's attention for a suitable period of time on the mystery concerned, before moving into vocal prayer. A discovery of the importance of silence is one of the secrets of practicing contemplation and meditation. One drawback of a society dominated by technology and the mass media is the fact that silence becomes increasingly difficult to achieve. Just as moments of silence are recommended in the Liturgy, so too in the recitation of the Rosary it is fitting to pause briefly after listening to the word of God, while the mind focuses on the content of a particular mystery.

The "Our Father"

After listening to the word and focusing on the mystery, it is natural for the mind to be lifted up towards the Father. In each of his mysteries, Jesus always leads us to the Father, for as he rests in the Father's bosom[6] he is continually turned towards him. He wants us to share in his intimacy with the Father, so that we can say with him: "Abba, Father".[7] By virtue of his relationship to the Father he makes

---

[6] cf. John 1:18
[7] Romans 8:15; Galatians 4:6

us brothers and sisters of himself and of one another, communicating to us the Spirit which is both his and the Father's. Acting as a kind of foundation for the Christological and Marian meditation which unfolds in the repetition of the *Hail Mary*, the *Our Father* makes meditation upon the mystery, even when carried out in solitude, an ecclesial experience.

The Ten "Hail Marys"

This is the most substantial element in the Rosary and also the one which makes it a Marian prayer par excellence. Yet when the Hail Mary is properly understood, we come to see clearly that its Marian character is not opposed to its Christological character, but that it actually emphasizes and increases it. The first part of the *Hail Mary*, drawn from the words spoken to Mary by the Angel Gabriel and by Saint Elizabeth, is a contemplation in adoration of the mystery accomplished in the Virgin of Nazareth. These words express, so to speak, the wonder of heaven and earth; they could be said to give us a glimpse of God's own wonderment as he contemplates his "masterpiece" – the Incarnation of the Son in the womb of the Virgin Mary. If we recall how, in the Book of Genesis, God "saw all that he had made,"[8] we can find here an echo of that "pathos with which God, at the dawn of creation, looked upon the work of his hands."[9] The repetition of the Hail Mary in the Rosary gives us a share in

---

[8] Genesis 1:31
[9] St. John Paul II, *Letter to Artists* (4 April 1999), 1: AAS 91 (1999), 1155.

God's own wonder and pleasure: in jubilant amazement we acknowledge the greatest miracle of history. Mary's prophecy here finds its fulfillment: "Henceforth all generations will call me blessed."[10]   —

The center of gravity in the *Hail Mary*, the hinge as it were which joins its two parts, is the name of Jesus. Sometimes, in hurried recitation, this center of gravity can be overlooked, and with it the connection to the mystery of Christ being contemplated. Yet it is precisely the emphasis given to the name of Jesus and to his mystery that is the sign of a meaningful and fruitful recitation of the Rosary. Pope Paul VI drew attention, in his Apostolic *Exhortation Marialis Cultus*, to the custom in certain regions of highlighting the name of Christ by the addition of a clause referring to the mystery being contemplated.[11] This is a praiseworthy custom, especially during public recitation. It gives forceful expression to our faith in Christ, directed to the different moments of the Redeemer's life. It is at once a profession of faith and an aid in concentrating our meditation, since it facilitates the process of assimilation to the mystery of Christ inherent in the repetition of the Hail Mary. When we repeat the name of Jesus — the only name given to us by which we may hope for salvation[12] — in close association with the name of his Blessed Mother, almost as if it were done at her suggestion, we set out on a path of

---

[10] Luke 1:48

[11] Cf. No. 46: AAS 66 (1974), 155. This custom has also been praised by the Congregation for Divine Worship and for the Discipline of the Sacraments in its *Direttorio su pietà popolare e liturgia. Principi e orientamenti* (17 December 2001), 201, Vatican City, 2002, 165.

[12] cf. Acts 4:12

assimilation meant to help us enter more deeply into the life of Christ.

From Mary's uniquely privileged relationship with Christ, which makes her the Mother of God, *Theotókos*, derives the forcefulness of the appeal we make to her in the second half of the prayer, as we entrust to her maternal intercession our lives and the hour of our death.

The "Gloria"

Trinitarian doxology is the goal of all Christian contemplation. For Christ is the way that leads us to the Father in the Spirit. If we travel this way to the end, we repeatedly encounter the mystery of the three divine Persons, to whom all praise, worship and thanksgiving are due. It is important that the Gloria, the high-point of contemplation, be given due prominence in the Rosary. In public recitation it could be sung, as a way of giving proper emphasis to the essentially Trinitarian structure of all Christian prayer.

To the extent that meditation on the mystery is attentive and profound, and to the extent that it is enlivened – from one Hail Mary to another – by love for Christ and for Mary, the glorification of the Trinity at the end of each decade, far from being a perfunctory conclusion, takes on its proper contemplative tone, raising the mind as it were to the heights of heaven and enabling us in some way to relive the experience of Tabor, a foretaste of the contemplation yet to come: "It is good for us to be here!"[13]

The Concluding Short Prayer

In current practice, the Trinitarian doxology is followed by a brief concluding prayer which varies according to local custom. Without in any way diminishing the value of such invocations, it is worthwhile to note that the contemplation of the mysteries could better express their full spiritual fruitfulness if an effort were made to conclude each mystery with a prayer for the fruits specific to that particular mystery. In this way the Rosary would better express its connection with the Christian life. One fine liturgical prayer suggests as much, inviting us to pray that, by meditation on the mysteries of the Rosary, we may come to "imitate what they contain and obtain what they promise."[14]

Such a final prayer could take on a legitimate variety of forms, as indeed it already does. In this way the Rosary can be better adapted to different spiritual traditions and different Christian communities. It is to be hoped, then, that appropriate formulas will be widely circulated, after due pastoral discernment and possibly after experimental use in centers and shrines particularly devoted to the Rosary, so that the People of God may benefit from an abundance of

---

[13] Luke 9:33

[14] "...*concede, quaesumus, ut haec mysteria sacratissimo beatae Mariae Virginis Rosario recolentes, et imitemur quod continent, et quod promittunt assequamur.*" Missale Romanum 1960, in festo B.M. Virginis a Rosario.

authentic spiritual riches and find nourishment for their personal contemplation.

The Rosary Beads

The traditional aid used for the recitation of the Rosary is the set of beads. At the most superficial level, the beads often become a simple counting mechanism to mark the succession of *Hail Marys*. Yet they can also take on a symbolism which can give added depth to contemplation.

Here the first thing to note is the way *the beads converge upon the Crucifix*, which both opens and closes the unfolding sequence of prayer. The life and prayer of believers is centered upon Christ. Everything begins from him, everything leads towards him, everything, through him, in the Holy Spirit, attains to the Father.

As a counting mechanism, marking the progress of the prayer, the beads evoke the unending path of contemplation and of Christian perfection. Blessed Bartolo Longo saw them also as a "chain" which links us to God. A chain, yes, but a sweet chain; for sweet indeed is the bond to God who is also our Father. A "filial" chain which puts us in tune with Mary, the "handmaid of the Lord"[15] and, most of all, with Christ himself, who, though he was in the form of God, made himself a "servant" out of love for us.[16]

---

[15] Luke 1:38
[16] Philippians 2:7

A fine way to expand the symbolism of the beads is to let them remind us of our many relationships, of the bond of communion and fraternity which unites us all in Christ.

The Opening and Closing

At present, in different parts of the Church, there are many ways to introduce the Rosary. In some places, it is customary to begin with the opening words of Psalm 70: "O God, come to my aid; O Lord, make haste to help me", as if to nourish in those who are praying a humble awareness of their own insufficiency. In other places, the Rosary begins with the recitation of the Creed, as if to make the profession of faith the basis of the contemplative journey about to be undertaken. These and similar customs, to the extent that they prepare the mind for contemplation, are all equally legitimate. The Rosary is then ended with a prayer for the intentions of the Pope, as if to expand the vision of the one praying to embrace all the needs of the Church. It is precisely in order to encourage this ecclesial dimension of the Rosary that the Church has seen fit to grant indulgences to those who recite it with the required dispositions.

If prayed in this way, the Rosary truly becomes a spiritual itinerary in which Mary acts as Mother, Teacher and Guide, sustaining the faithful by her powerful intercession. Is it any wonder, then, that the soul feels the need, after saying this prayer and experiencing so profoundly the motherhood of Mary, to burst forth in praise of the Blessed Virgin, either in that splendid prayer the Salve Regina or in the Litany of Loreto? This is the crowning moment of an inner journey which has brought the faithful into living contact with the mystery of Christ and his Blessed Mother.

Distribution Over Time

The Rosary can be recited in full every day, and there are those who most laudably do so. In this way it fills with prayer the days of many a contemplative, or keeps company with the sick and the elderly who have abundant time at their disposal. Yet it is clear – and this applies all the more if the new series of *mysteria lucis* is included – that many people will not be able to recite more than a part of the Rosary, according to a certain weekly pattern. This weekly distribution has the effect of giving the different days of the week a certain spiritual "color", by analogy with the way in which the Liturgy colors the different seasons of the liturgical year.

According to current practice, Monday and Thursday are dedicated to the "Joyful Mysteries", Tuesday and Friday to the "Sorrowful Mysteries", and Wednesday, Saturday and Sunday to the "Glorious Mysteries". Where might the "Mysteries of Light" be inserted? If we consider that the "glorious mysteries" are said on both Saturday and Sunday, and that Saturday has always had a special Marian flavor, the second weekly meditation on the "Joyful Mysteries", mysteries in which Mary's presence is especially pronounced, could be moved to Saturday. Thursday would then be free for meditating on the "Mysteries of Light".

This indication is not intended to limit a rightful freedom in personal and community prayer, where account needs to be taken of spiritual and pastoral needs and of the occurrence of particular liturgical celebrations which might call for suitable adaptations. What is really important is that the Rosary should always be seen and experienced as a path of contemplation. In the Rosary, in a way similar to what takes place in the Liturgy, the Christian week, centered on Sunday, the day of Resurrection, becomes a journey through the mysteries of the life of Christ, and he is revealed in the lives of his disciples as the Lord of time and of history.

Part Two:
The Glorious Mysteries

From the Apostolic Letter of Saint John Paul II entitled Rosarium Virginis Mariae:

"The contemplation of Christ's face cannot stop at the image of the Crucified One. He is the Risen One!"[17] The Rosary has always expressed this knowledge born of faith and invited the believer to pass beyond the darkness of the Passion in order to gaze upon Christ's glory in the Resurrection and Ascension. Contemplating the Risen One, Christians rediscover the reasons for their own faith[18] and relive the joy not only of those to whom Christ appeared – the Apostles, Mary Magdalene and the disciples on the road to Emmaus – but also the joy of Mary, who must have had an equally intense experience of the new life of her glorified Son. In the Ascension, Christ was raised in glory to the right hand of the Father, while Mary herself would be raised to that same glory in the Assumption, enjoying beforehand, by a unique privilege, the destiny reserved for all the just at the resurrection of the dead. Crowned in glory – as she appears in the last glorious mystery – Mary shines forth as Queen of

---

[17] John Paul II, Apostolic Letter *Novo Millennio Ineunte* (6 January 2001), 28: AAS 93 (2001), 284.
[18] cf. 1Corinthians 15:14

the Angels and Saints, the anticipation and the supreme realization of the eschatological state of the Church.

At the center of this unfolding sequence of the glory of the Son and the Mother, the Rosary sets before us the third glorious mystery, Pentecost, which reveals the face of the Church as a family gathered together with Mary, enlivened by the powerful outpouring of the Spirit and ready for the mission of evangelization. The contemplation of this scene, like that of the other glorious mysteries, ought to lead the faithful to an ever greater appreciation of their new life in Christ, lived in the heart of the Church, a life of which the scene of Pentecost itself is the great "icon". The glorious mysteries thus lead the faithful to greater hope for the eschatological goal towards which they journey as members of the pilgrim People of God in history. This can only impel them to bear courageous witness to that "good news" which gives meaning to their entire existence.

Chapter 1:
The Resurrection

Saint John Paul II gave the following address on Wednesday, May 21, 1997 during his General Audience:

Mary was witness to whole paschal mystery

After Jesus had been laid in the tomb, Mary "alone remains to keep alive the flame of faith, preparing to receive the joyful and astonishing announcement of the Resurrection."[19] The expectation felt on Holy Saturday is one of the loftiest moments of faith for the Mother of the Lord: in the darkness that envelops the world, she entrusts herself fully to the God of life, and thinking back to the words of her Son, she hopes in the fulfillment of the divine promises.

The Gospels mention various appearances of the risen Christ, but not a meeting between Jesus and his Mother. This silence must not lead to the conclusion that after the Resurrection Christ did not appear to Mary; rather it invites us to seek the reasons why the Evangelists made such a choice.

On the supposition of an "omission", this silence could be attributed to the fact that what is necessary for our saving knowledge

---

[19] *Address at the General Audience*, 3 April 1996; *L'Osservatore Romano* English edition, 10 April 1996, p. 7.

was entrusted to the word of those "chosen by God as witnesses,"[20] that is, the Apostles, who gave their testimony of the Lord Jesus' Resurrection "with great power."[21] Before appearing to them, the Risen One had appeared to several faithful women because of their ecclesial function: "Go and tell my brethren to go to Galilee, and there they will see me."[22]

If the authors of the New Testament do not speak of the Mother's encounter with her risen Son, this can perhaps be attributed to the fact that such a witness would have been considered too biased by those who denied the Lord's Resurrection, and therefore not worthy of belief.

Furthermore, the Gospels report a small number of appearances by the risen Jesus and certainly not a complete summary of all that happened during the 40 days after Easter. Saint Paul recalls that he appeared "to more than 500 brethren at one time."[23] How do we explain the fact that an exceptional event known to so many is not mentioned by the Evangelists? It is an obvious sign that other appearances of the Risen One were not recorded, although they were among the well-known events that occurred.

---

[20] Acts 10:41
[21] cf. Acts 4:33
[22] Matthew 28:10
[23] 1 Corinthians 15:6

How could the Blessed Virgin, present in the first community of disciples,[24] be excluded from those who met her divine Son after he had risen from the dead?

Indeed, it is legitimate to think that the Mother was probably the first person to whom the risen Jesus appeared. Could not Mary's absence from the group of women who went to the tomb at dawn[25] indicate that she had already met Jesus? This inference would also be confirmed by the fact that the first witnesses of the Resurrection, by Jesus' will, were the women who had remained faithful at the foot of the Cross and therefore were more steadfast in faith.

Indeed, the Risen One entrusts to one of them, Mary Magdalene, the message to be passed on to the Apostles.[26] Perhaps this fact too allows us to think that Jesus showed himself first to his Mother, who had been the most faithful and had kept her faith intact when put to the test.

Lastly, the unique and special character of the Blessed Virgin's presence at Calvary and her perfect union with the Son in his suffering on the Cross seem to postulate a very particular sharing on her part in the mystery of the Resurrection.

A fifth-century author, Sedulius, maintains that in the splendor of his risen life Christ first showed himself to his mother. In fact, she, who at the Annunciation was the way he entered the world, was called to spread the marvelous news of the Resurrection in order to

---

[24] cf. Acts 1:14
[25] cf. Mark 16:1; Matthew 28:1
[26] cf. John 20:17-18

become the herald of his glorious coming. Thus bathed in the glory of the Risen One, she anticipates the Church's splendor.[27]

It seems reasonable to think that Mary, as the image and model of the Church which waits for the Risen One and meets him in the group of disciples during his Easter appearances, had had a personal contact with her risen Son, so that she too could delight in the fullness of paschal joy.

Present at Calvary on Good Friday[28] and in the Upper Room on Pentecost,[29] the Blessed Virgin too was probably a privileged witness of Christ's Resurrection, completing in this way her participation in all the essential moments of the paschal mystery. Welcoming the risen Jesus, Mary is also a sign and an anticipation of humanity, which hopes to achieve its fulfilment through the resurrection of the dead.

In the Easter season, the Christian community addresses the Mother of the Lord and invites her to rejoice: "*Regina Caeli, laetare. Alleluia!*". "Queen of heaven, rejoice. Alleluia!" Thus it recalls Mary's joy at Jesus' Resurrection, prolonging in time the "rejoice" that the Angel addressed to her at the Annunciation, so that she might become a cause of "great joy" for all people.

---

[27] cf. Sedulius, *Paschale carmen*, 5, 357-364, CSEL 10, 140f
[28] cf. John 19:25
[29] cf. Acts 1:14

Chapter 2:
The Ascension

Saint John Paul II gave the following homily on the Solemnity of the Ascension of Our Lord, May 24, 1979:

Dear sons and brothers and friends in Jesus Christ,

With joy then and fresh resolves for the future, let us reflect briefly on the great mystery of today's liturgy. In the Scripture readings the whole significance of Christ's Ascension is summarized for us. The richness of this mystery is spelled out in two statements: Jesus gave instructions, and then Jesus took his place.

In the providence of God – in the eternal design of the Father – the hour had come for Christ to go away. He would leave his Apostles behind, with his Mother Mary, but only after he had given them his instructions. The Apostles now had a mission to perform according to the instructions that Jesus left, and these instructions were in turn the faithful expression of the Father's will.

The instructions indicated, above all, that the Apostles were to wait for the Holy Spirit, who was the gift of the Father. From the beginning, it had to be crystal-clear that the source of the Apostles' strength is the Holy Spirit. It is the Holy Spirit who guides the Church in the way of truth; the Gospel is to spread through the power of God, and not by means of human wisdom or strength.

The Apostles, moreover, were instructed to teach – to proclaim the Good News to the whole world. And they were to baptize in the name of the Father, and of the Son, and of the Holy Spirit. Like Jesus, they were to speak explicitly about the Kingdom of God and about salvation. The Apostles were to give witness to Christ to the ends of the earth. The early Church clearly understood these instructions and the missionary era began. And everybody knew that this missionary era could never end until the same Jesus, who went up to heaven, would come back again.

The words of Jesus became a treasure for the Church to guard and to proclaim, to meditate on and to live. And at the same time, the Holy Spirit implanted in the Church an apostolic charism, in order to keep this revelation intact. Through his words Jesus was to live on in his Church: I am with you always. And so the whole ecclesial community became conscious of the need for fidelity to the instructions of Jesus, to the deposit of faith. This solicitude was to pass from generation to generation – down to our own day. And it was because of this principle that I spoke recently to your own Rectors, stating that the first priority for seminaries today is the teaching of God's word in all its purity and integrity, with all its exigencies and in all its power. The word of God – and the word of God alone – is the basis for all ministry, for all pastoral activity, for all priestly action.

The power of God's word constituted the dynamic basis of the Second Vatican Council, and John XXIII pointed out clearly on the day it opened: 'The greatest concern of the Ecumenical Council is this: that the sacred deposit of Christian doctrine should be more

effectively guarded and taught'. And if the seminarians of this generation are to be adequately prepared to take on the heritage and challenge of this Council they must be trained above all in God's word:
in 'the sacred deposit of Christian doctrine' Yes, dear sons, our greatest challenge is to be faithful to the instructions of the Lord Jesus.

And the second reflection on the meaning of the Ascension is
found in this phrase: Jesus took his place. After having undergone
the humiliation of his passion and death, Jesus took his place at the
right-hand of God; he took his place with his eternal Father. But he
also entered heaven as our Head. Whereupon, in the expression of
Leo the Great, the glory of the Head became the hope of the body.
For all eternity Christ takes is place as the firstborn among many
brethren: our nature is with God in Christ. And as man, the Lord
Jesus lives for ever to intercede for us with Father. At the same time,
from his throne of glory, Jesus sends out to the whole Church a message of hope and a call to holiness.

Because of Christ's merits, because of his intercession with the
Father, we are able to attain justice and holiness of life, in him. The
Church may indeed experience difficulties, the Gospel may suffer
setbacks, but because Jesus is at the right-hand of the Father the
Church will never know defeat. Christ's victory is ours. The power of
the glorified Christ, the beloved Son of the eternal Father, is supera-
bundant, to sustain each of us and all of us in the fidelity of our dedication to God's Kingdom and in the generosity of our celibacy. The
efficacy of Christ's Ascension touches all us in the concrete reality of
our daily lives. Because of this mystery it is the vocation of the whole

Church to wait in joyful hope for the coming of our Savior, Jesus Christ.

Dear sons, be imbued with the hope that is so much a part of the mystery of the Ascension of Jesus. Be deeply conscious of Christ's victory and triumph over sin and death. Realize that the strength of Christ is greater than our weakness, greater than the weakness of the whole world. Try to understand and share the joy that Mary experienced in knowing that her Son had taken his place with his Father, whom he loved infinitely. And renew your faith today in the promise of our Lord Jesus Christ, who has gone to prepare a place for us, so that he can come back again and take us to himself.

This is the mystery of the Ascension of our Head. Let us always remember: Jesus gave instructions, and then Jesus took his place. Amen.

Chapter 3:
Pentecost

Saint John Paul II gave the following homily on the Solemnity of the Pentecost, Sunday, May 31, 1998:

Credo in Spiritum Sanctum, Dominum et vivificantem: I believe in the Holy Spirit, the Lord, the Giver of life.

With the words of the Nicene-Constantinopolitan Creed, the Church proclaims her faith in the Paraclete; a faith that is born of the apostolic experience of Pentecost. The passage from the Acts of the Apostles, which today's liturgy has offered for our meditation, recalls in fact the marvels worked on the day of Pentecost, when with great astonishment the Apostles saw Jesus' words come true. As was mentioned in the passage from St John's Gospel proclaimed a few moments ago, on the eve of his Passion he had assured them: "I will pray the Father and he will give you another Counsellor, to be with you forever."[30] This "Counselor, the Holy Spirit, whom the Father will send in my name, he will teach you all things, and bring to your remembrance all that I have said to you."[31]

And the Holy Spirit, coming down upon them with extraordinary power, enabled them to proclaim the teaching of Christ Jesus to the whole world. Their courage was so great, their determination so sure, that they were prepared to do anything, even to give up their life. The gift of the Spirit had released their deepest energies, concentrating them on the mission entrusted to them by the Redeemer. And it will be the Counselor, the *Parakletos*, who will guide them in preaching the Gospel to all. The Spirit will teach them the whole truth, drawing it from the wealth of Christ's word, so that, in turn, they may communicate it to people in Jerusalem and the rest of the world.

How can we not give thanks to God for the wonders the Spirit has never ceased to accomplish in these two millenniums of Christian life? Indeed, the event of grace at Pentecost has continued to bear its marvellous fruits, everywhere instilling apostolic zeal, a desire for contemplation, the commitment to live and serve God and our brothers and sisters with complete dedication. Today too, the Spirit sustains great and small acts of forgiveness and prophecy in the Church and gives life to ever new charisms and gifts, which attest to his ceaseless action in human hearts. [...]

---

[30] John 14:16
[31] John 14:26

Veni, Sancte Spiritus!

The magnificent sequence, which contains a rich theology of the Holy Spirit, would also be worthy of meditation, stanza by stanza. Here we will reflect only on the first word: *Veni*, come! It recalls the waiting of the Apostles after Christ's Ascension into heaven.

In the Acts of the Apostles, Luke presents them to us gathered in the Upper Room in prayer with the Mother of Jesus.[32] What better words than these could express their prayer: *"Veni, Sancte Spiritus"* — the invocation, that is, of the one who moved over the face of the waters at the beginning of the world,[33] whom Jesus had promised them as the Paraclete?

The hearts of Mary and the Apostles at those moments were longing for his coming, alternating between ardent faith and the confession of human inadequacy. The Church's piety has interpreted and passed on this sentiment in the hymn *"Veni, Sancte Spiritus"*. The Apostles know that the work Christ has entrusted to them is arduous, but decisive for the history of humanity's salvation. Will they be able to complete it? The Lord reassures their hearts. At every step of the mission that will lead them to proclaim and witness to the Gospel to the furthest corners of the globe, they will be able to count on the Spirit promised by Christ. The Apostles, recalling Christ's promise on the days between the Ascension and Pentecost, will focus their every thought and sentiment on that *veni* — come!

---

[32] cf. Acts 1:14
[33] cf. Genesis 1:2

Veni, Sancte Spiritus! Thus beginning her invocation to the Holy Spirit, the Church makes her own the substance of the Apostles' prayer as they gathered with Mary in the Upper Room; indeed, she extends it in history and makes it ever timely.

Veni, Sancte Spiritus! Thus she says over and over in every corner of the earth, her fervor unchanged, firmly aware that she must remain in the Upper Room, always awaiting the Spirit. At the same time, she knows that she must leave the Upper Room and travel the world's roads, with the ever new task of bearing witness to the mystery of the Spirit.

Veni, Sancte Spiritus! So we pray with Mary, sanctuary of the Holy Spirit, a most precious dwelling-place of Christ among us, so that she may help us to be living temples of the Spirit and tireless witnesses of the Gospel.

Veni, Sancte Spiritus! Veni, Sancte Spiritus! Veni, Sancte Spiritus! Amen!

Chapter 4:
The Assumption of Mary

*Saint John Paul II gave the following homily on the 8th **World Youth Day** in Denver, Colorado, on the Solemnity of the Assumption of the Blessed Virgin Mary, Sunday, August 15, 1993:*

"God who is mighty has done, great things for me."[34]

Beloved Young People and Dear Friends in Christ,

Today the Church finds herself, with Mary, on the threshold of the house of Zechariah in Ain–Karim. With new life stirring within her, the Virgin of Nazareth hastened there, immediately after the Fiat of the Annunciation, to be of help to her cousin Elizabeth.

It was Elizabeth who first recognized the "great things" which God was doing in Mary. Filled with the Holy Spirit, Elizabeth marveled that the mother of her Lord should come to her.[35] With deep insight into the mystery, she declared: "Blest is she who believed that the Lord's words to her would be fulfilled."[36] With her soul full of

---

[34] Luke 1:49
[35] Luke 1:43
[36] Luke 1:45

humble gratitude to God, Mary replied with a hymn of praise: "God who is mighty has done great things for me and holy is his name."[37]

On this Feast the Church celebrates the culmination of the "great things" which God has done in Mary: her glorious Assumption into Heaven. And throughout the Church the same hymn of thanksgiving, the "Magnificat", rings out as it did for the first time at Ain–Karim: "All generations call you blessed."[38]

Gathered at the foot of the Rocky Mountains, which remind us that Jerusalem too was surrounded by hills[39] and that Mary had gone up into those hills,[40] we are here to celebrate Mary's "going up" to the heavenly Jerusalem, to the threshold of the eternal Temple of the Most Holy Trinity. Here in Denver, at the "World Youth Day", the Catholic sons and daughters of America, together with others "from every tribe and tongue, people and nation,"[41] join all the generations since who have cried out: God has done great things for you, Mary – and for all of us, members of his pilgrim people![42]

With my heart full of praise for the Queen of Heaven, the sign of hope and source of comfort on our pilgrimage of faith to "the heavenly Jerusalem",[43] I greet all of you who are present at this Solemn Liturgy. It is a pleasure for me to see so many priests, Religious and lay faithful from Denver, from the State of Colorado, from all

[37] Luke 1:49
[38] Luke 1:48
[39] Psalm 124:2
[40] Luke 1:39
[41] Luke 1:39
[42] Luke 1:49
[43] Hebrews 12:22

parts of the United States, and from so many countries of the world, who have joined the young people of the World Youth Day to honor the definitive victory of grace in Mary, the Mother of the Redeemer.

The Eighth "World Youth Day" is a celebration of Life. This gathering has been the occasion of a serious reflection on the words of Jesus Christ: "I came that they may have life, and have it abundantly."[44] Young people from every corner of the world, in ardent prayer you have opened your hearts to the truth of Christ's promise of new Life. Through the Sacraments, especially Penance and the Eucharist, and by means of the unity and friendship created among so many, you have had a real and transforming experience of the new Life which only Christ can give. You, young pilgrims, have also shown that you understand that Christ's gift of Life is not for you alone. You have become more conscious of your vocation and mission in the Church and in the world. For me, our meeting has been a deep and moving experience of your faith in Christ, and I make my own the words of Saint Paul: "I have great confidence in you, I have great pride in you; I am filled with encouragement, I am overflowing with joy."[45]

These are not words of empty praise. I am confident that you have grasped the scale of the challenge that lies before you, and that you will have the wisdom and courage to meet that challenge. So much depends on you.

---

[44] John 10:10
[45] 2 Corinthians 7:4

This marvelous world – so loved by the Father that he sent his only Son for its salvation[46] – is the theater of a never – ending battle being waged for our dignity and identity as free, spiritual beings. This struggle parallels the apocalyptic combat described in the First Reading of this Mass. Death battles against Life: a "culture of death" seeks to impose itself on our desire to live, and live to the full. There are those who reject the light of life, preferring "the fruitless works of darkness."[47] Their harvest is injustice, discrimination, exploitation, deceit, violence. In every age, a measure of their apparent success is the death of the Innocents. In our own century, as at no other time in history, the "culture of death" has assumed a social and institutional form of legality to justify the most horrible crimes against humanity: genocide, "final solutions", "ethnic cleansings", and the massive "taking of lives of human beings even before they are born, or before they reach the natural point of death."[48]

Today's Reading from the Book of Revelation presents the Woman surrounded by hostile forces. The absolute nature of their attack is symbolized in the object of their evil intention: the Child, the symbol of new life. The "dragon",[49] the "ruler of this world",[50] and the "father of lies",[51] relentlessly tries to eradicate from human hearts the sense of gratitude and respect for the original, extraordi-

---

[46] John 3:17
[47] Ephesians 5:11
[48] *Dominum et vivificantem*, 57
[49] Revelation 12:3
[50] John 12:31
[51] John 8:44

nary and fundamental gift of God: human life itself. Today that struggle has become increasingly direct.

Dear Friends, this gathering in Denver on the theme of Life should lead us to a deeper awareness of the internal contradiction present in a part of the culture of the modern "metropolis".

When the Founding Fathers of this great nation enshrined certain inalienable rights in the Constitution – and something similar exists in many countries and in many International Declarations – they did so because they recognized the existence of a "law" – a series of rights and duties – engraved by the Creator on each person's heart and conscience.

In much of contemporary thinking, any reference to a "law" guaranteed by the Creator is absent. There remains only each individual's choice of this or that objective as convenient or useful in a given set of circumstances. No longer is anything considered intrinsically "good" and "universally binding". Rights are affirmed but, because they are without any reference to an objective truth, they are deprived of any solid basis. Vast sectors of society are confused about what is right and what is wrong, and are at the mercy of those with the power to "create" opinion and impose it on others.

The family especially is under attack. And the sacred character of human life denied. Naturally, the weakest members of society are the most at risk: the unborn, children, the sick, the handicapped, the old, the poor and unemployed, the immigrant and refugee, the South of the world!

Mary's Assumption & The Battle for Life

Young pilgrims, Christ needs you to enlighten the world and to show it the "path to life".[52] The challenge is to make the Church's "yes" to Life concrete and effective. The struggle will be long, and it needs each one of you. Place your intelligence, your talents, your enthusiasm, your compassion and your fortitude at the service of life!

Have no fear. The outcome of the battle for Life is already decided, even though the struggle goes on against great odds and with much suffering. This certainty is what the Second Reading declares: "Christ is now raised from the dead, the first fruits of those who have fallen asleep. ...so in Christ all will come to life again."[53] The paradox of the Christian message is this: Christ – the Head – has already conquered sin and death. Christ in his Body – the pilgrim People of God – continually suffers the onslaught of the Evil One and all the evil which sinful humanity is capable of.

At this stage of history, the liberating message of the Gospel of Life has been put into your hands. And the mission of proclaiming it to the ends of the earth is now passing to your generation. Like the great Apostle Paul, you too must feel the full urgency of the task: "Woe to me if I do not evangelize".[54] Woe to you if you do not succeed in defending life. The Church needs your energies, your enthusiasm, your youthful ideals, in order to make the Gospel of Life penetrate the fabric of society, transforming people's hearts and the

---

[52] Psalm 16:11
[53] 1 Corinthians 15:20-22
[54] 1 Corinthians 9:16

structures of society in order to create a civilization of true justice and love. Now more than ever, in a world that is often without light and without the courage of noble ideals, people need the fresh, vital spirituality of the Gospel.

Do not be afraid to go out on the streets and into public places, like the first Apostles who preached Christ and the Good News of salvation in the squares of cities, towns and villages. This is no time to be ashamed of the Gospel.[55] It is the time to preach it from the rooftops.[56] Do not be afraid to break out of comfortable and routine modes of living, in order to take up the challenge of making Christ known in the modern "metropolis". It is you who must "go out into the byroads"[57] and invite everyone you meet to the banquet which God has prepared for his people. The Gospel must not be kept hidden because of fear or indifference. It was never meant to be hidden away in private. It has to be put on a stand so that people may see its light and give praise to our heavenly Father.

Jesus went in search of the men and women of his time. He engaged them in an open and truthful dialogue, whatever their condition. As the Good Samaritan of the human family, he came close to people to heal them of their sins and of the wounds which life inflicts, and to bring them back to the Father's house. Young people of "World Youth Day", the Church asks you to go, in the power of the Holy Spirit, to those who are near and those who are far away. Share

---

[55] Romans 1:16
[56] Matthew 10:27
[57] Matthew 22:9

with them the freedom you have found in Christ. People thirst for genuine inner freedom. They yearn for the Life which Christ came to give in abundance. The world at the approach of a new millennium, for which the whole Church is preparing, is like a field ready for the harvest. Christ needs laborers ready to work in his vineyard. May you, the Catholic young people of the world, not fail him. In your hands, carry the Cross of Christ. On your lips, the words of Life. In your hearts, the saving grace of the Lord.

The Blessed Mother is "Taken up to Life"

At her Assumption, Mary was "taken up to Life" – body and soul. She is already a part of "the first fruits"[58] of our Savior's redemptive Death and Resurrection. The Son took his human life from her; in return he gave her the fullness of communion in Divine Life. She is the only other being in whom the mystery has already been completely accomplished. In Mary the final victory of Life over death is already a reality. And, as the Second Vatican Council teaches: "In the most holy Virgin the Church has already reached the perfection whereby she exists without spot or wrinkle."[59] In and through the Church we too have hope of "an inheritance which is imperishable, undefiled, and unfading, kept in heaven for us."[60]

---

[58] 1 Corinthians 15:20
[59] *Lumen gentium*, 65
[60] 1 Peter 1:4

You are blessed, O Mary! Mother of the Eternal Son born of your virgin womb, you are full of grace.[61] You have received the abundance of Life[62] as no one else among the descendants of Adam and Eve. As the most faithful "hearer of the Word",[63] you not only treasured and pondered this mystery in your heart,[64] but you observed it in your body and nourished it by the self–giving love with which you surrounded Jesus throughout his earthly life. As Mother of the Church, you guide us still from your place in heaven and intercede for us. You lead us to Christ, "the Way, and the Truth, and the Life",[65] and help us to increase in holiness by conquering sin.[66]

The Liturgy presents you, Mary, as the Woman clothed with the sun.[67] But you are even more splendidly clothed with that Divine Light which can become the Life of all those created in the image and likeness of God himself: "this life was the light of the human race; the light shines in the darkness, and the darkness has not overcome it."[68]

O woman clothed with the sun, the youth of the world greet you with so much love; they come to you with all the courage of their young hearts. Denver has helped them to become more conscious of the Life which your Divine Son has brought.

---

[61] Luke 1:28
[62] John 10:10
[63] Luke 11:28
[64] Luke 11:2,19,51
[65] John 14:16
[66] *Lumen gentium*, 65
[67] Revelation 12:1
[68] John 1:4-5

We are all witnesses of this.

These young people now know that Life is more powerful than the forces of death; they know that the Truth is more powerful than darkness; that Love is stronger than death.[69]

Your spirit rejoices, O Mary, and our spirit rejoices with you because the Mighty One has done great things for you and for us, – for all these young people gathered here in Denver, for all of us, for all the young people of the world, for all the young people, this generation, the future generation. The Mighty One has done great things for you, Mary, and for us. For you and for us, for us with you. The Mighty One – and holy is his name!

His mercy is from age to age.

We rejoice, Mary, we rejoice with you, Virgin assumed into heaven.

The Lord has done great things for you! The Lord has done great things for us! Alleluia. Amen.

---

[69] Cant 8:6

Chapter 5:
The Coronation of the Mary

Saint John Paul II gave the following homily on the Solemnity of the Assumption of the Blessed Virgin Mary, Sunday, August 15, 1998:

"Blessed is she who believed that there would be a fulfilment of what was spoken to her from the Lord."[70]

With these words, Elizabeth welcomes Mary who has come to pay her a visit. This same beatitude resounds in heaven and on earth, from generation to generation (cf. Lk 1:48), and particularly in today's solemn celebration. Mary is blessed because she immediately believed in the Lord's Word, because she unquestioningly accepted the Almighty's will revealed to her by the angel at the Annunciation.

We could see in Mary's journey from Nazareth to Ain-Karin, recounted in today's Gospel, a prefiguration as it were of her unique spiritual journey which, beginning with her "yes" on the day of the Annunciation, is crowned by her Assumption into heaven in body and soul. A journey to God, ever illumined and sustained by faith.

---

[70] Luke 1:45

The Second Vatican Council says that Mary "advanced in her pilgrimage of faith, and faithfully persevered in her union with her Son unto the Cross."[71] For this reason, she so pleased the King of the universe in her incomparable beauty that now, fully associated with him in body and in soul, she is resplendent as the Queen standing at his right hand.[72] [...]

In today's solemnity, the liturgy invites us all to contemplate Mary as the "woman clothed with the sun, with the moon under her feet, and on her head a crown of twelve stars."[73] In her shines forth Christ's victory over Satan, described in apocalyptic terms as the "great red dragon."[74]

This glorious and at the same time dramatic vision reminds the Church in all the ages of her destiny of light in the kingdom of heaven, and of comfort in the trials she must bear during her earthly pilgrimage. As long as this world endures, history will always be the theatre of the clash between God and Satan, between good and evil, between grace and sin, between life and death.

The events of this century, now drawing to a close, also witness with extraordinary eloquence to the depth of this struggle that marks the history of peoples, but also the hearts of every man and woman. However, the Easter proclamation which has just resounded in the

---

[71] *Lumen gentium*, n. 58
[72] St. John Paul II is here quoting from the Responsorial Psalm recited during the Solemnity on this date.
[73] Revelation 12:1
[74] Revelation 12:3

Apostle Paul's words,[75] lays the foundation of sure hope for everyone. Mary most holy, taken up into heaven, is a luminous icon of this mystery and hope.

In this second year of immediate preparation for the Great Jubilee of the Year 2000, I have wished to invite believers to be more attentive to the presence and action of the Holy Spirit and to "a renewed appreciation of the theological virtue of hope."[76]

Mary, glorified in her body, appears today as the star of hope for the Church and for humanity on its way towards the third Christian millennium. Her sublime exaltation does not distance her from her people or from the world's problems, on the contrary, it enables her to watch effectively over human affairs with that attentive concern with which she obtained the first miracle from Jesus at the wedding in Cana.

Revelation says that the woman clothed with the sun "was with child and she cried out in her pangs of birth, in anguish for delivery."[77] This calls to mind a text of the Apostle Paul which has fundamental importance for the Christian theology of hope. "We know", we read in his Letter to the Romans, "that the whole creation has been groaning in travail together until now; and not only the creation, but we ourselves, who have the first fruits of the Spirit, groan

---

[75] cf. 1 Cor 15:20
[76] *Tertio millennio adveniente*, n. 46
[77] Revelation 12:2

inwardly as we wait for adoption as sons, the redemption of our bodies. For in this hope we were saved."[78]

As we celebrate her Assumption into heaven in body and soul, we pray to Mary to help the men and women of our time to live in this world with faith and hope, seeking God's kingdom in all things; may she help believers to be open to the presence and action of the Holy Spirit, the Creator and Renewer Spirit, who can transform hearts; may she enlighten our minds on the destiny that awaits us, the dignity of every person and the nobility of the human body.

Mary, taken up into heaven, show yourself to everyone as Mother of hope! Show yourself to everyone as Queen of the civilization of love!

---

[78] Romans 8:22-24

Part Three:
The Joyful Mysteries

From the Apostolic Letter of Saint John Paul II entitled Rosarium Virginis Mariae:

The first five decades, the "Joyful Mysteries", are marked by the joy radiating from the event of the Incarnation. This is clear from the very first mystery, the Annunciation, where Gabriel's greeting to the Virgin of Nazareth is linked to an invitation to messianic joy: "Rejoice, Mary". The whole of salvation history, in some sense the entire history of the world, has led up to this greeting. If it is the Father's plan to unite all things in Christ,[79] then the whole of the universe is in some way touched by the divine favor with which the Father looks

---

[79] cf. Ephesians 1:10

upon Mary and makes her the Mother of his Son. The whole of humanity, in turn, is embraced by the fiat with which she readily agrees to the will of God.

Exultation is the keynote of the encounter with Elizabeth, where the sound of Mary's voice and the presence of Christ in her womb cause John to "leap for joy."[80] Gladness also fills the scene in Bethlehem, when the birth of the divine Child, the Saviour of the world, is announced by the song of the angels and proclaimed to the shepherds as "news of great joy."[81]

The final two mysteries, while preserving this climate of joy, already point to the drama yet to come. The Presentation in the Temple not only expresses the joy of the Child's consecration and the ecstasy of the aged Simeon; it also records the prophecy that Christ will be a "sign of contradiction" for Israel and that a sword will pierce his mother's heart.[82] Joy mixed with drama marks the fifth mystery, the finding of the twelve-year-old Jesus in the Temple. Here he appears in his divine wisdom as he listens and raises questions, already in effect one who "teaches". The revelation of his mystery as the Son wholly dedicated to his Father's affairs proclaims the radical nature of the Gospel, in which even the closest of human relationships are challenged by the absolute demands of the Kingdom. Mary and Joseph, fearful and anxious, "did not understand" his words.[83]

---

[80] cf. Luke 1:44
[81] Luke 2:10
[82] cf. Luke 2:34-35
[83] Luke 2:50

To meditate upon the "joyful" mysteries, then, is to enter into the ultimate causes and the deepest meaning of Christian joy. It is to focus on the realism of the mystery of the Incarnation and on the obscure foreshadowing of the mystery of the saving Passion. Mary leads us to discover the secret of Christian joy, reminding us that Christianity is, first and foremost, *evangelion*, "good news", which has as its heart and its whole content the person of Jesus Christ, the Word made flesh, the one Savior of the world.

Chapter 1:
The Annunciation

*Saint John Paul II gave the following homily in Nazareth during his Jubilee Pilgrimage to the Holy Land, while celebrating Mass in the **Basilica of the Annunciation**, Saturday, March 25, 2000:*

"Behold the handmaid of the Lord. Be it done unto me according to your word."[84]

... On this day the eyes of the whole Church turn to Nazareth. I have longed to come back to the town of Jesus, to feel once again, in contact with this place, the presence of the woman of whom Saint Augustine wrote: "He chose the mother he had created; he created the mother he had chosen."[85] Here it is especially easy to understand why all generations call Mary blessed.[86]

... We are gathered to celebrate the great mystery accomplished here two thousand years ago. The Evangelist Luke situates the event clearly in time and place: "In the sixth month, the angel Gabriel was sent by God to a town in Galilee called Nazareth, to a virgin betrothed to a man named Joseph. . . The virgin's name was Mary."[87]

---

[84] Quoting from the Angelus Prayer, Luke 1:38
[85] *Sermo* 69, 3, 4
[86] cf. Luke 2:48
[87] Luke 1:26-27

Figure 1: Pope John Paul II kneeling at the altar of the Basilica of the Annunciation, Nazareth

Figure 2: Basilica of the Annunciation, Exterior

But in order to understand what took place in Nazareth two thousand years ago, we must return to the Reading from the Letter to the Hebrews. That text enables us, as it were, to listen to a conversation between the Father and the Son concerning God's purpose from all eternity. "You who wanted no sacrifice or oblation prepared a body for me. You took no pleasure in holocausts or sacrifices for sin. Then I said ...? God, here I am! I am coming to obey your will."[88] The Letter to the Hebrews is telling us that, in obedience to the Father's will, the Eternal Word comes among us to offer the sacrifice which surpasses all the sacrifices offered under the former

---

[88] Hebrews 10:5-7

Covenant. His is the eternal and perfect sacrifice which redeems the world.

The divine plan is gradually revealed in the Old Testament, particularly in the words of the Prophet Isaiah which we have just heard: "The Lord himself will give you a sign. It is this: the virgin is with child and will soon give birth to a child whom she will call Emmanuel."[89] Emmanuel - God with us. In these words, the unique event that was to take place in Nazareth in the fullness of time is foretold, and it is this event that we are celebrating here with intense joy and happiness.

Our Jubilee Pilgrimage has been a journey in spirit, which began in the footsteps of Abraham, "our father in faith."[90] That journey has brought us today to Nazareth, where we meet Mary, the truest daughter of Abraham. It is Mary above all others who can teach us what it means to live the faith of "our father". In many ways, Mary is clearly different from Abraham; but in deeper ways "the friend of God" and the young woman of Nazareth are very alike.[91]

Both receive a wonderful promise from God. Abraham was to be the father of a son, from whom there would come a great nation. Mary is to be the Mother of a Son who would be the Messiah, the Anointed One. "Listen!" Gabriel says, "You are to conceive and bear

---

[89] Isaiah 7:14
[90] Roman Canon; cf. Romans 4:11-12
[91] cf. Isaiah 41:8

a son ... The Lord God will give him the throne of his ancestor David ... and his reign will have no end."[92]

For both Abraham and Mary, the divine promise comes as something completely unexpected. God disrupts the daily course of their lives, overturning its settled rhythms and conventional expectations. For both Abraham and Mary, the promise seems impossible. Abraham's wife Sarah was barren, and Mary is not yet married: "How can this come about", she asks, "since I am a virgin?"[93]

Like Abraham, Mary is asked to say yes to something that has never happened before. Sarah is the first in the line of barren wives in the Bible who conceive by God's power, just as Elizabeth will be the last. Gabriel speaks of Elizabeth to reassure Mary: "Know this too: your kinswoman Elizabeth has, in her old age, herself conceived a son."[94]

Like Abraham, Mary must walk through darkness, in which she must simply trust the One who called her. Yet even her question, "How can this come about?" suggests that Mary is ready to say yes, despite her fears and uncertainties. Mary asks not whether the promise is possible, but only how it will be fulfilled. It comes as no surprise, therefore, when finally she utters her fiat: "I am the handmaid of the Lord. Let what you have said be done to me."[95] With these words, Mary shows herself the true daughter of Abraham, and she becomes the Mother of Christ and Mother of all believers.

---

[92] Luke 1:31-33
[93] Luke 1:34
[94] Luke 1:36
[95] Luke 1:38

In order to penetrate further into the mystery, let us look back to the moment of Abraham's journey when he received the promise. It was when he welcomed to his home three mysterious guests,[96] and offered them the adoration due to God: *tres vidit et unum adoravit*. That mysterious encounter foreshadows the Annunciation, when Mary is powerfully drawn into communion with the Father, the Son and the Holy Spirit. Through the fiat that Mary uttered in Nazareth, the Incarnation became the wondrous fulfillment of Abraham's encounter with God. So, following in the footsteps of Abraham, we have come to Nazareth to sing the praises of the woman "through whom the light rose over the earth."[97]

But we have also come to plead with her. What do we, pilgrims on our way into the Third Christian Millennium, ask of the Mother of God? Here in the town which Pope Paul VI, when he visited Nazareth, called "the school of the Gospel", where "we learn to look at and to listen to, to ponder and to penetrate the deep and mysterious meaning of the very simple, very humble and very beautiful appearing of the Son of God,"[98] I pray, first, for a great renewal of faith in all the children of the Church. A deep renewal of faith: not just as a general attitude of life, but as a conscious and courageous profession of the Creed: "*Et incarnatus est de Spiritu Sancto ex Maria Virgine, et homo factus est.*"

---

[96] cf. Genesis 18:1-15
[97] Hymn "Ave Regina Caelorum"
[98] Address in Nazareth, January 5, 1964

In Nazareth, where Jesus "grew in wisdom and age and grace before God and men,"[99] I ask the Holy Family to inspire all Christians to defend the family against so many present-day threats to its nature, its stability and its mission. To the Holy Family, I entrust the efforts of Christians and of all people of good will to defend life and to promote respect for the dignity of every human being.

To Mary, the *Theotókos*, the great Mother of God, I consecrate the families of the Holy Land, the families of the world.

In Nazareth where Jesus began his public ministry, I ask Mary to help the Church everywhere to preach the "good news" to the poor, as he did.[100] In this "year of the Lord's favor", I ask her to teach us the way of humble and joyful obedience to the Gospel in the service of our brothers and sisters, without preferences and without prejudices.

"O Mother of the Word Incarnate, despise not my petitions, but in your mercy hear and answer me. Amen."[101]

---

[99] Luke 2:52
[100] cf. Luke 4:18
[101] Memorare prayer

Chapter 2:
The Visitation

From the papal encyclical of Saint John Paul II, Redemptoris Mater,
"On the Blessed Virgin Mary, in the life of the Pilgrim Church," Part Two,
"Blessed is She Who Believed":

Immediately after the narration of the Annunciation, the Evangelist Luke guides us in the footsteps of the Virgin of Nazareth towards "a city of Judah."[102] According to scholars this city would be the modern Ain Karim, situated in the mountains, not far from Jerusalem. Mary arrived there "in haste," to visit Elizabeth her kinswoman. The reason for her visit is also to be found in the fact that at the Annunciation Gabriel had made special mention of Elizabeth, who in her old age had conceived a son by her husband Zechariah, through the power of God: "your kinswoman Elizabeth in her old age has also conceived a Son; and this is the sixth month with her who was called barren. For with God nothing will be impossible."[103] The divine messenger had spoken of what had been accomplished in Elizabeth in order to answer Mary's question. "How shall this be, since I have no husband?"[104] It is to come to pass precisely through

---

[102] Luke 1:39
[103] Luke 1:36-37
[104] Luke 1:34

the "power of the Most High," just as it happened in the case of Elizabeth, and even more so.

Moved by charity, therefore, Mary goes to the house of her kinswoman. When Mary enters, Elizabeth replies to her greeting and feels the child leap in her womb, and being "filled with the Holy Spirit" she greets Mary with a loud cry: "Blessed are you among women, and blessed is the fruit of your womb!"[105] Elizabeth's exclamation or acclamation was subsequently to become part of the Hail Mary, as a continuation of the angel's greeting, thus becoming one of the Church's most frequently used prayers. But still more significant are the words of Elizabeth in the question which follows: "And why is this granted me, that the mother of my Lord should come to me?"[106] Elizabeth bears witness to Mary: she recognizes and proclaims that before her stands the Mother of the Lord, the Mother of the Messiah. The son whom Elizabeth is carrying in her womb also shares in this witness: "The babe in my womb leaped for joy."[107] This child is the future John the Baptist, who at the Jordan will point out Jesus as the Messiah.

While every word of Elizabeth's greeting is filled with meaning, her final words would seem to have fundamental importance: "And blessed is she who believed that there would be a fulfillment of what was spoken to her from the Lord."[108] These words can be linked with the little "full of grace" of the angel's greeting. Both of these

---

[105] cf. Luke 1:40-42
[106] Luke 1:43
[107] Luke 1:44
[108] Luke 1:45

texts reveal an essential Mariological content, namely the truth about Mary, who has become really present in the mystery of Christ precisely because she "has believed." The fullness of grace announced by the angel means the gift of God himself. Mary's faith, proclaimed by Elizabeth at the Visitation, indicates how the Virgin of Nazareth responded to this gift.

As the Council teaches, "'The obedience of faith' must be given to God who reveals, an obedience by which man entrusts his whole self freely to God."[109] This description of faith found perfect realization in Mary. The "decisive" moment was the Annunciation, and the very words of Elizabeth: "And blessed is she who believed" refer primarily to that very moment.

---

[109] Romans 16:26; *cf.* Rom. 1:5; 2 Cor. 10:5-6

Chapter 3:
The Nativity

Urbi et Orbi message of Saint John Paul II, Christmas 2003:

Descendit de caelis Salvator mundi. Gaudeamus!

The Saviour of the world has come down from heaven. Let us rejoice!

This proclamation, filled with deep rejoicing,

echoed in the night of Bethlehem.

Today the Church renews it with unchanged joy:

the Saviour is born for us!

A wave of tenderness and hope fills our hearts,

together with an overpowering need for closeness and peace.

In the crib we contemplate the One

who stripped himself of divine glory

in order to become poor, driven by love for mankind.

Beside the crib the Christmas tree,

with its twinkling lights,

reminds us that with the birth of Jesus

the tree of life has blossomed anew in the desert of humanity.

The crib and the tree: precious symbols,

which hand down in time the true meaning of Christmas!

In the heavens there echoes the proclamation of the angels:
"To you is born in the city of David
a Saviour, who is Christ the Lord."[110]
What wonder!
By being born in Bethlehem, the Eternal Son of God
has entered into the history of each person
living on the face of the earth.
He is now present in the world
as the one Saviour of humanity
For this reason we pray to him:
Saviour of the world, save us!

Save us from the great evils which rend humanity
in these first years of the third millennium.
Save us from the wars and armed conflicts
which lay waste whole areas of the world,
from the scourge of terrorism
and from the many forms of violence
which assail the weak and the vulnerable.
Save us from discouragement
as we face the paths to peace,
difficult paths indeed, yet possible and therefore necessary;
paths which are always and everywhere urgent,
especially in the Land where You were born,

---

[110] Luke 2:11

the Prince of Peace.

And you, Mary, *the Virgin of expectation and fulfillment,*
who hold the secret of Christmas,
make us able to recognize in the Child
whom you hold in your arms the heralded Saviour,
who brings hope and peace to all.
With you we worship him and trustingly say:
we need You, Redeemer of man,
You who know the hopes and fears of our hearts.
Come and stay with us, Lord!
May the joy of your Nativity reach
to the farthest ends of the universe!

Chapter 4:
The Presentation of
Jesus at the Temple

Saint John Paul II gave the following homily on the Feast of the Presentation of Jesus in the Temple, February 2, 1998:

Lumen ad revelationem gentium![111]

These words resound in the temple of Jerusalem, as 40 days after the birth of Jesus, Mary and Joseph prepare to "present him to the Lord."[112] By emphasizing the contrast between the modest, humble action of the two parents and the glory of the event as perceived by Simeon and Anna, the Evangelist Luke apparently wants to suggest that the temple itself is waiting for the Child's coming. In fact, in the prophetic attitude of the two elderly people, the entire Old Covenant expresses the joy of the meeting with the Redeemer.

Simeon and Anna go to the temple both longing for the Messiah, both inspired by the Holy Spirit, as Mary and Joseph take Jesus there in obedience to the precepts of the law. At the sight of the Child, they sense that it is truly he, the Awaited One, and Simeon, as if in ecstasy, proclaims: "Lord, now let your servant depart in peace,

---

[111] "Light for revelation to the Gentiles," Luke 2:32
[112] Luke 2:22

according to your word; for my eyes have seen your salvation which your have prepared in the presence of all peoples, a light for revelation to the Gentiles, and for glory to your people Israel."[113]

Lumen ad revelationem gentium!

With his inspired words, Simeon, a man of the Old Covenant, a man of the temple of Jerusalem, expresses his conviction that this Light is meant not only for Israel, but also for pagans and all the peoples of the earth. With him, the "aged" world receives in its arms the splendor of God's eternal "youth". However, the shadow of the Cross already looms in the background, because the darkness will reject that Light. Indeed, turning to Mary, Simeon prophesies: "This child is set for the fall and rising of many in Israel, and for a sign that is spoken against (and a sword will pierce through your own soul also), that thoughts out of many hearts may be revealed."[114]

Lumen ad revelationem gentium!

The words of Simeon's canticle ring out in many temples of the New Covenant, where every evening Christ's disciples finish the Liturgy of the Hours by praying Compline. In this way the Church, the people of the New Covenant, takes as it were the last word of the Old Covenant and proclaims the fulfilment of the divine promise, announcing that the "light for revelation to the Gentiles" has spread over all the earth and is present everywhere in Christ's redemptive work.

---

[113] Luke 2:29-32
[114] Luke 2:34-35

Together with the Canticle of Simeon, the Liturgy of the Hours has us repeat Christ's last words on the Cross: *In manus tuas, Domine, commendo spiritum meum* — "Father, into your hands I commend my spirit."[115] It also invites us to contemplate with wonder and gratitude the saving action of Christ, "light for revelation to the Gentiles", for the sake of mankind: *Redemisti nos, Domine, Deus veritatis* — "You have redeemed us, Lord, God of truth".

In this way the Church proclaims the fulfilment of the world's Redemption, awaited by the prophets and announced by Simeon in the temple of Jerusalem.

Lumen ad revelationem gentium!

Today, with our lighted candles, we too go to meet him who is "the Light of the world" and we welcome him in his Church with the full enthusiasm of our baptismal faith. Everyone who sincerely professes this faith is promised the final, definitive "meeting" with the Lord in his kingdom. In Polish tradition, as well in that of other nations, these blessed candles have a special meaning because, after they have been brought home, they are lit in times of danger, during storms and disasters, as a sign of entrusting oneself, one's family and all one possesses to God's protection. This is the reason why these candles are called *gromnice* in Polish, that is, candles which avert lightning and protect against evil, and why this feast is called Candlemas (literally: St Mary of the Candles ["gromnice"]).

---

115 *cf.* Luke 23:46

Even more eloquent is the custom of putting the candle blessed on this day in the hands of a Christian on his deathbed, that it may illumine his last steps on the way to eternity. This practice is meant to show that, by following the light of faith, the dying person is waiting to enter the eternal dwelling place, where there is no longer "need of light of lamp or sun, for the Lord God will be their light."[116]

Today's responsorial psalm also refers to this entry into the kingdom of light: "Lift up, O gates, your lintels; reach up, you ancient portals, that the Lord of glory may come in."[117]

These words refer directly to Jesus Christ, who enters the temple of the Old Covenant in his parents' arms, but we can also apply them to every believer who crosses the threshold of eternity, carried in the arms of the Church. Believers accompany his last journey by praying: "Let perpetual light shine on him!", so that the angels and saints may welcome him, and Christ, Redeemer of man, may surround him with his eternal light.

Dear brothers and sisters, today we celebrate the Second Day of Consecrated Life, which is meant to arouse renewed concern in the Church for the gift of vocations to the consecrated life. Dear men and women religious, dear members of secular institutes and societies of apostolic life, the Lord has called you to follow him in a closer and more exceptional way! In our times, dominated by secularism and materialism, by your total and definitive gift of self to Christ you are a sign of an alternative life to the logic of the world, because it is rad-

---

[116] *cf.* Revelation 22:5
[117] Psalm 23[24]:7

ically inspired by the Gospel and oriented to future eschatological realities. Always remain faithful to this special vocation!

... The lighted candles carried by each person in the first part of this solemn liturgy show the watchful expectation of the Lord which should mark every believer's life, and particularly the life of those whom the Lord calls to a special mission in the Church. They are a strong reminder to bear witness in the world to Christ, the light that never fades: "Let your light so shine before men, that they may see your good works and give glory to your Father who is in heaven."[118]

Dear brothers and sisters, may your total fidelity to the poor, chaste and obedient Christ be a source of light and hope for everyone you meet.

Lumen ad revelationem gentium!

May Mary, who was prompt in obedience, courageous in poverty and receptive in fruitful virginity as she fulfilled the Father's will, obtain from Jesus that "all who have received the gift of following him in the consecrated life may be enabled to bear witness to that gift by their transfigured lives, as they joyfully make their way with all their brothers and sisters towards our heavenly homeland and the light that will never grow dim."[119]

Praised be Jesus Christ!

---

[118] Matthew 5:16
[119] *Vita consecrata*, n. 112

Chapter 5:
The Finding of Jesus in the Temple

Saint John Paul II gave the following address on Wednesday, January 15, 1997 during his General Audience:

Mary co-operates by personal obedience

The Evangelist Luke describes the young Jesus' pilgrimage to the temple in Jerusalem as the last episode of the infancy narrative, before the start of John the Baptist's preaching. It is an usual occasion which sheds light on the long years of his hidden life in Nazareth.

On this occasion, with his strong personality Jesus reveals that he is aware of his mission, giving to this second "entry" into his "Father's house" the meaning of his total gift of self to God which had already marked his presentation in the temple.

This passage seems to contrast with Luke's note that Jesus was obedient to Joseph and Mary.[120] But, if one looks closely, here he seems to put himself in a conscious and almost deliberate antithesis to his normal state as son, unexpectedly causing a definite separation from Mary and Joseph. As his rule of conduct, Jesus states that he

---

[120] *cf.* Luke 2:51

belongs only to the Father and does not mention the ties to his earthly family. Jesus' behavior seemed very unusual

Through this episode, Jesus prepares his Mother for the mystery of the Redemption. During those three dramatic days when the Son withdraws from them to stay in the temple, Mary and Joseph experience an anticipation of the triduum of his Passion, Death and Resurrection.

Letting his Mother and Joseph depart for Galilee without telling them of his intention to stay behind in Jerusalem, Jesus brings them into the mystery of that suffering which leads to joy, anticipating what he would later accomplish with his disciples through the announcement of his Passover.

According to Luke's account, on the return journey to Nazareth Mary and Joseph, after a day's traveling, are worried and anguished over the fate of the Child Jesus. They look for him in vain among their relatives and acquaintances. Returning to Jerusalem and finding him in the temple, they are astonished to see him "sitting among the teachers, listening to them and asking them questions."[121] His behavior seems most unusual. Certainly for his parents, finding him on the third day means discovering another aspect of his person and his mission.

He takes the role of teacher, as he will later do in his public life, speaking words that arouse admiration: "And all who heard him were

---

[121] Luke 2:46

astounded at his understanding and his answers."[122] Revealing a wisdom that amazes his listeners, he begins to practise the art of dialogue that will be a characteristic of his saving mission.

His Mother asked Jesus: "Son, why have you treated us so? Behold, your father and I have been looking for you anxiously."[123] Here we can discern an echo of the "whys" asked by so many mothers about the suffering their children cause them, as well as the questions welling up in the heart of every man and woman in times of trial.

Jesus' reply, in the form of a question, is highly significant: "How is it that you sought me? Did you not know that I must be in my Father's house?"[124]

With this response, he discloses the mystery of his person to Mary and Joseph in an unexpected, unforeseen way, inviting them to go beyond appearances and unfolding before them new horizons for his future.

In his reply to his anguished Mother, the Son immediately reveals the reason for his behavior. Mary had said: "Your father," indicating Joseph; Jesus replies: "My Father", meaning the heavenly Father.

Referring to his divine origin, he does not so much want to state that the temple, his Father's house, is the natural "place" for his presence, as that he must be concerned about all that regards his Fa-

---

122 Luke 2:47
123 Luke 2:48
124 Luke 2:49

ther and his plan. He means to stress that his Father's will is the only norm requiring his obedience.

This reference to his total dedication to God's plan is highlighted in the Gospel text by the words: "I must be", which will later appear in his prediction of the Passion.[125]

His parents then are asked to let him go and carry out his mission wherever the heavenly Father will lead him.

The Evangelist comments: "And they did not understand the saying which he spoke to them."[126] Mary and Joseph do not perceive the sense of his answer, nor the way (apparently a rejection) he reacts to their parental concern. With this attitude, Jesus intends to reveal the mysterious aspects of his intimacy with the Father, aspects which Mary intuits without knowing how to associate them with the trial she is undergoing.

Luke's words teach us how Mary lives this truly unusual episode in the depths of her being. She "kept all these things in her heart."[127] The Mother of Jesus associates these events with the mystery of her Son, revealed to her at the Annunciation, and ponders them in the silence of contemplation, offering her co-operation in the spirit of a renewed "fiat".

In this way the first link is forged in a chain of events that will gradually lead Mary beyond the natural role deriving from her motherhood, to put herself at the service of her divine Son's mission.

---

[125] *cf.* Mark 8:31
[126] Luke 2:50
[127] Luke 2:51

At the temple in Jerusalem, in this prelude to his saving mission, Jesus associates his Mother with himself; no longer is she merely the One who gave him birth, but the Woman who, through her own obedience to the Father's plan, can co-operate in the mystery of Redemption.

Thus keeping in her heart an event so charged with meaning, Mary attains a new dimension of her co-operation in salvation.

Part Four:
The Sorrowful Mysteries

From the Apostolic Letter of Saint John Paul II entitled Rosarium Virginis Mariae:

The Gospels give great prominence to the Sorrowful Mysteries of Christ. From the beginning Christian piety, especially during the Lenten devotion of the Way of the Cross, has focused on the individual moments of the Passion, realizing that here is found *the culmination of the revelation of God's love* and the source of our salvation. The Rosary selects certain moments from the Passion, inviting the faithful to contemplate them in their hearts and to relive them. The sequence of meditations begins with Gethsemane, where Christ experiences a moment of great anguish before the will of the Father, against which the weakness of the flesh would be tempted to rebel. There Jesus encounters all the temptations and confronts all the sins of humanity, in order to say to the Father: "Not my will but yours be done."[128] This "Yes" of Christ reverses the "No" of our first parents in the Garden of Eden. And the cost of this faithfulness to the Father's will is made clear in the following mysteries; by his scourging, his crowning with thorns, his carrying the Cross and his death on the Cross, the Lord is cast into the most abject suffering: Ecce homo!

---

[128] Luke 22:42 and parallels

This abject suffering reveals not only the love of God but also the meaning of man himself.

Ecce homo: the meaning, origin and fulfillment of man is to be found in Christ, the God who humbles himself out of love "even unto death, death on a cross."[129] The sorrowful mysteries help the believer to relive the death of Jesus, to stand at the foot of the Cross beside Mary, to enter with her into the depths of God's love for man and to experience all its life-giving power.

---

[129] Philippians 2:8

Chapter 1:
The Agony in the Garden

Saint John Paul II gave the following address on Wednesday, April 11, 1979 during his General Audience:

Evangelization is carried out with the help of words. And just the words spoken by Christ during his passion have an enormous force of expression. It can also be said that they are a place for a special meeting with every man; they are the opportunity and the reason to manifest great solidarity. How often do we return to what the Evangelists recorded as the guiding thread of Christ's prayer in the garden of Olives? "My Father, if it be possible, let this cup pass from me."[130] Does not every man say so? Does not every man feel like this in suffering, in tribulation, before the cross?: "Let it pass from me..." How much deep human truth is contained in this sentence! Christ, as a real man, felt aversion to suffering: "He began to be sorrowful and troubled"[131] and said: "Let it pass from me..."; let it not come, let it not reach me! It is necessary to accept the whole human expression, the whole human truth of these words, in order to be able to unite them with those of Christ: "If it is possible, let this cup pass from

---

130 Matthew 26:39
131 Matthew 26:37

me; nevertheless, not as I will, but as thou wilt!"[132] Every man, confronted by suffering, is faced with a challenge... Is this only a challenge of fate? Christ gives the answer, saying: "As thou wilt." He does not address fate, a "blind fate". He speaks to God, to the Father. Sometimes this answer is not enough for us, because it is not the last word, but the first. We cannot understand either Gethsemane or Calvary unless in the context of the whole paschal event, of the whole mystery.

In the words of Christ's passion there is a particularly intense meeting of the "human" with the "divine". The Gethsemane words already show this. Later on Christ will rather be silent. He will say a sentence to Judas. Then to those brought by Judas to the Garden of Gethsemane to arrest Him. Then again to Peter. Before the Sanhedrin he does not defend himself, but bears witness. And so also before Pilate. Before Herod, on the other hand, "he made no answer."[133] During the infliction of the sentence, the words of Isaiah come true: "like a lamb that is led to the slaughter, and like a sheep that before its shearers is dumb, so he opened not his mouth."[134] His last words fall from the cross.

They can be explained as a whole by the course of the event, by the horrible torture and, at the same time, through them, in spite of their brevity and conciseness, there appears what is "divine" and "salvific". We feel the "salvific" significance of the words addressed

---

[132] Matthew 26:39
[133] Luke 23:9
[134] Isaiah 53:7

to his Mother, to John, to the good thief, as also the words referring to the crucifiers. The last words addressed to the Father are overwhelming: the last echo and at the same time almost the continuation of the Gethsemane prayer. Christ says: "My God, my God, why hast thou forsaken me?"[135] repeating the Psalmist's words.[136] At Gethsemane he had said: "If it be possible, let this cup pass from me."[137] And now, from the cross, he has publicly confirmed that the "cup" has not been removed, that he must drink it to the dregs. Such is the Father's will. In fact, this last word: "It is finished"[138] is an echo of the Gethsemane prayer. And, finally, only these: "Father, into thy hands I commit my spirit."[139]

Christ's agony. First the moral agony at Gethsemane. Then the agony, at once moral and physical, on the cross. No one has expressed so deeply as Christ the human torment of dying, just because he was the Son of God; because in him the "human" and the "divine" constituted a mysterious unity. Therefore also those words of Christ's passion, so penetratingly human, will remain forever a revelation of the "divinity" which in Christ is bound up with humanity, in the fullness of personal unity. It can be said: the death of God-Man was necessary, in order that we, heirs to original sin, might see what the drama in man's death is.

---

[135] Matthew 27:46
[136] cf. Psalm 21
[137] Matthew 26:39
[138] John 19:30
[139] Luke 23:46

Chapter 2:
The Scourging at the Pillar

Following the Scourging at the Pillar, Pontius Pilate presented the scourged, bloody, and beaten Jesus to the crowds, saying *"Ecce homo!* Behold the Man!"

Saint John Paul II gave the following address "To the University Professors of All Nations" on Saturday, September 9, 2000:

... You never cease to enquire into the value of the human person. Each of you could say, with the ancient philosopher: "I am searching for man!"

Among the many responses given to this fundamental quest, you have accepted that given by Christ, a response which emerges from his words but which is seen even before shining brightly on his face. *Ecce homo*: Behold the man![140] In showing Christ's battered face to the frenzied crowd, Pilate did not imagine that he would, in a sense, speak a word of revelation. Unwittingly, he pointed out to the world the One in whom all human beings can recognize their origin, and in whom all can hope to find their salvation. *Redemptor hominis*:

---

[140] John 19:5

this is the image of Christ which, from my first Encyclical, I have sought to "shout" to the world, and which this Jubilee year seeks to propose anew to human minds and hearts.

Figure 3: *Ecce Homo* by Antonio Ciseri

Chapter 3:
The Crowning with Thorns

Saint John Paul II gave the following address for the Angelus on Sunday, November 26, 1978:

Today is the feast of Christ the King of the universe.

While I was thinking what to say to you today, beloved Brothers and Sisters gathered for the "Angelus", it came into my mind that the words of the Gospel of St John should ring out in the first place here—yes, in this very place, in front of the facade of St. Peter's Basilica, in the heart of Rome.

Pilate said: "Are you the King of the Jews?" Jesus answered: "Do you say this of your own accord, or did others say it to you about me?" Pilate answered, "Am I a Jew? Your own nation and the chief priests have handed you over to me; what have you done?" Jesus answered, "My kingship is not of this world."[141]

These words remind us of past events, which took place in the distant outskirts of the great Roman Empire. They are not, however, without significance. Perhaps present-day, topical problems still resound in them. In this dialogue, perhaps, there could be found, at

---

[141] John 18:33-36

least from certain standpoints, the same discussions that happen today.

Christ answers the judge's question and shows that the accusation brought against him is groundless. He does not aim at temporal power.

Shortly afterwards he will be scourged and crowned with thorns. He will be mocked and insulted, with the words: "Hail, King of the Jews!"[142] But Jesus is silent, as if he wished, by his silence, to express to the end what he had already replied to Pilate.

But this was not yet the complete answer. And Pilate felt it. And for this reason he asked for the second time: "So you are a king?"[143]

A strange question, strange after all that Christ had declared so firmly. But Pilate felt that the accused man's denial did not exhaust everything: in the depth of this denial an affirmation was hidden. What? And here Christ helps Pilate, the judge, to find it:

"You say that I am a king. For this I was born, and for this I have come into the world, to bear witness to the truth. Everyone who is of the truth hears my voice."[144]

We must all reflect carefully on Christ's denial and affirmation.

Jesus' affirmation does not belong to the trial that was once held in the distant territories of the Roman Empire, but is always at

---

[142] John 19:3
[143] John 18:37
[144] John 18:37

the center of our lives. It is relevant today. Those who issue laws, and those who govern states and those who judge, must think it over.

Every Christian, every man, who is always a citizen, and who consequently belongs to a definite political, ,economic, national and international community, must reflect on this affirmation.

"For this I was born, and for this I have come into the world, to bear .witness to the truth." Christ the King says this before the court of the governor-judge, while waiting for the sentence that would be passed shortly afterwards.

In this connection let us listen again to what the Second Vatican Council said: "The Church, by reason of her role and competence, is not identified with any political community nor bound by ties to any political system. It is at once the sign and the safeguard of the transcendental dimension of the human person."'[145]

This is how the contemporary Church thinks and speaks.

The Church wishes to be faithful to what Christ said.

This is her *raison d'etre*.

In this connection, we think of those brothers of ours, who are tried, and perhaps condemned to death—if not to physical death, at least to civil death—because they profess their faith, because they are faithful to truth, because they defend real justice.

It must be recognized that, unfortunately, similar situations are not lacking also in the world of today. On this day of Christ the King, it is necessary, therefore, to stress the resemblance of those

---

[145] *Gaudium et Spes*, 76

who are undergoing them, with Christ himself, tried and condemned before the court of Pilate.

Let us pray every day: Thy Kingdom come.

Chapter 4:
The Carrying of the Cross

Saint John Paul II gave the following Mediation and Prayers on the Fifth Station of the Cross at the Roman Colosseum on Good Friday 2000:

V/. We adore you, O Christ, and we bless you.

R/. Because by your holy Cross you have redeemed the world.

Simon of Cyrene helps Jesus to carry his Cross

They compelled Simon.[146]

The Roman soldiers did this because they feared that in his exhaustion the Condemned Man would not be able to carry the Cross as far as Golgotha. Then they would not be able to carry out the sentence of crucifixion.

They were looking for someone to help carry the Cross.

Their eyes fell on Simon. They compelled him to take the weight upon his shoulders. We can imagine that Simon did not want to do this and objected. Carrying the cross together with a convict could be considered an act offensive to the dignity of a free man.

---

[146] cf. Mark 15:21

Although unwilling, Simon took up the Cross to help Jesus.

In a Lenten hymn we hear the words: "Under the weight of the Cross Jesus welcomes the Cyrenean." These words allow us to discern a total change of perspective: the divine Condemned One is someone who, in a certain sense, "makes a gift" of his Cross.

Was it not he who said: "He who does not take up his cross and follow me is not worthy of me"?[147]

Simon receives a gift.

He has become "worthy" of it.

What the crowd might see as an offence to his dignity has, from the perspective of redemption, given him a new dignity.

In a unique way, the Son of God has made him a sharer in his work of salvation.

Is Simon aware of this?

The evangelist Mark identifies Simon of Cyrene as the "father of Alexander and Rufus."[148]

If the sons of Simon of Cyrene were known to the first Christian community, it can be presumed that Simon too, while carrying the Cross, came to believe in Christ. From being forced, he freely accepted, as though deeply touched by the words: "Whoever does not carry his cross with me is not worthy of me."

By his carrying of the Cross, Simon was brought to the knowledge of the gospel of the Cross.

---

[147] Matthew 10:38
[148] 15:21

Since then, this gospel has spoken to many, countless Cyreneans, called in the course of history to carry the cross with Jesus.

Prayer

O Christ, you gave to Simon of Cyrene
the dignity of carrying your Cross.
Welcome us too under its weight,
welcome all men and women
and grant to everyone the gift of readiness to serve.
Do not permit that we should turn away from those
who are crushed by the cross of illness
loneliness, hunger or injustice.
As we carry each other's burdens,
help us to become witnesses to the gospel of the Cross
and witnesses to you,
who live and reign for ever and ever.
R. Amen.

Stabat Mater:

Is there one who would not weep,
whelmed in miseries so deep,
Christ's dear Mother to behold?

Chapter 5:
The Death of Christ

Saint John Paul II gave the following Mediation and Prayers on the Twelfth Station of the Cross at the Roman Colosseum on Good Friday 2000:

Jesus dies on the Cross

V/. We adore you, O Christ, and we bless you.

R/. Because by your holy Cross you have redeemed the world.

Jesus dies on the Cross

"Father, forgive them, for they know not what they do."[149]

At the height of his Passion, Christ does not forget man, especially those who are directly responsible for his suffering. Jesus knows that more than anything else man needs love; he needs the mercy which at this moment is being poured out on the world.

"Truly, I say to you, today you will be with me in Paradise."[150]

This is how Jesus replies to the plea of the criminal hanging on his right: "Jesus, remember me when you come into your kingdom."[151]

---

[149] Luke 23:34
[150] Luke 23:43
[151] Luke 23:42

The promise of a new life. This is the first fruit of the Passion and imminent Death of Christ. A word of hope to man.

At the foot of the Cross stood Mary, and beside her the disciple, John the Evangelist. Jesus says: "Woman, behold your son!" and to the disciple: "Behold your mother!"[152]

"And from that moment the disciple took her to his own home."[153]

This is his bequest to those dearest to his heart.

His legacy to the Church.

The desire of Jesus as he dies is that the maternal love of Mary should embrace all those for whom he is giving his life, the whole of humanity.

Immediately after, Jesus cries out: "I thirst."[154] This word describes the dreadful burning which consumes his whole body.

It is the one word which refers directly to his physical suffering.

Then Jesus adds: "My God, my God, why have you abandoned me?"[155] These words of the Psalm are his prayer. Despite their tone, these words reveal the depths of his union with the Father.

In the last moments of his life on earth, Jesus thinks of the Father. From this moment on, the dialogue will only be between the dying Son and the Father who accepts his sacrifice of love.

---

[152] John 19:26-27
[153] John 19:27
[154] John 19:28
[155] Matthew 27:46; cf. Psalm 22:2

When the ninth hour comes, Jesus cries out: "It is accomplished!"[156]

Now the work of the redemption is complete.

The mission, for which he came on earth, has reached its goal.

The rest belongs to the Father:

"Father, into your hands I commit my spirit."[157]

And having said this, he breathed his last.

"The curtain of the temple was torn in two..."[158]

The "Holy of Holies" of the Jerusalem Temple is opened at the moment when it is entered by the Priest of the New and Eternal Covenant.

Prayer

Lord Jesus Christ,

in the moment of your agony

you were not indifferent to humanity's fate,

and with your last breath

you entrusted to the Father's mercy

the men and women of every age,

with all their weaknesses and sins.

Fill us and the generations yet to come

with your Spirit of love,

so that our indifference

---

[156] John 19:30
[157] Luke 23:46
[158] Matthew 27:51

will not render vain in us
the fruits of your death.

To you, crucified Jesus, the wisdom and the power of God,
be honour and glory for ever and ever.
R. Amen.

Stabat Mater:

She looked upon her sweet Son,
saw him hang in desolation,
till his spirit forth he sent.

Part Five:
The Luminous Mysteries

From the Apostolic Letter of Saint John Paul II entitled Rosarium Virginis Mariae:

Moving on from the infancy and the hidden life in Nazareth to the public life of Jesus, our contemplation brings us to those mysteries which may be called in a special way "mysteries of light". Certainly the whole mystery of Christ is a mystery of light. He is the "light of the world."[159] Yet this truth emerges in a special way during the years of his public life, when he proclaims the Gospel of the Kingdom. In proposing to the Christian community five significant moments – "luminous" mysteries – during this phase of Christ's life, I think that the following can be fittingly singled out: (1) his Baptism in the Jordan, (2) his self-manifestation at the wedding of Cana, (3) his proclamation of the Kingdom of God, with his call to conversion, (4) his Transfiguration, and finally, (5) his institution of the Eucharist, as the sacramental expression of the Paschal Mystery.

Each of these mysteries is a revelation of the Kingdom now present in the very person of Jesus. The Baptism in the Jordan is first of all a mystery of light. Here, as Christ descends into the waters, the

---

[159] John 8:12

innocent one who became "sin" for our sake,[160] the heavens open wide and the voice of the Father declares him the beloved Son,[161] while the Spirit descends on him to invest him with the mission which he is to carry out. Another mystery of light is the first of the signs, given at Cana,[162] when Christ changes water into wine and opens the hearts of the disciples to faith, thanks to the intervention of Mary, the first among believers. Another mystery of light is the preaching by which Jesus proclaims the coming of the Kingdom of God, calls to conversion[163] and forgives the sins of all who draw near to him in humble trust:[164] the inauguration of that ministry of mercy which he continues to exercise until the end of the world, particularly through the Sacrament of Reconciliation which he has entrusted to his Church.[165] The mystery of light par excellence is the Transfiguration, traditionally believed to have taken place on Mount Tabor. The glory of the Godhead shines forth from the face of Christ as the Father commands the astonished Apostles to "listen to him"[166] and to prepare to experience with him the agony of the Passion, so as to come with him to the joy of the Resurrection and a life transfigured by the Holy Spirit. A final mystery of light is the institution of the Eucharist, in which Christ offers his body and blood as food under

---

[160] cf. 2 Corinthians 5:21
[161] cf. Matthew 3:17 and parallels
[162] cf. John 2:1-12
[163] cf. Mark 1:15
[164] cf. Mark 2:3-13; Luke 7:47- 48
[165] cf. John 20:22-23
[166] cf. Luke 9:35 and parallels

the signs of bread and wine, and testifies "to the end" his love for humanity,[167] for whose salvation he will offer himself in sacrifice.

In these mysteries, apart from the miracle at Cana, the presence of Mary remains in the background. The Gospels make only the briefest reference to her occasional presence at one moment or other during the preaching of Jesus,[168] and they give no indication that she was present at the Last Supper and the institution of the Eucharist. Yet the role she assumed at Cana in some way accompanies Christ throughout his ministry. The revelation made directly by the Father at the Baptism in the Jordan and echoed by John the Baptist is placed upon Mary's lips at Cana, and it becomes the great maternal counsel which Mary addresses to the Church of every age: "Do whatever he tells you."[169] This counsel is a fitting introduction to the words and signs of Christ's public ministry, and it forms the Marian foundation of all the "mysteries of light".

---

[167] John 13:1
[168] cf. Mark 3:31-5; John 2:12
[169] John 2:5

Chapter 1:
The Baptism of Jesus

*Saint John Paul II gave the following homily at Wadi Al-Kharrar at the
River Jordan during his Jubilee Pilgrimage to the Holy Land on Tuesday, March
21, 2000:*

In the Gospel of Saint Luke we read that "the word of God
came to John the son of Zechariah in the wilderness; and he went
into all the region about the Jordan, preaching a baptism of repentance for the forgiveness of sins."[170] Here, at the River Jordan, where
both banks are visited by hosts of pilgrims honoring the Baptism of
the Lord, I too lift up my heart in prayer:

Glory to you, O Father, God of Abraham, Isaac and Jacob!
You sent your servants the Prophets
to speak your word of faithful love
and call your people to repentance.

On the banks of the River Jordan,
you raised up John the Baptist,
a voice crying in the wilderness,
sent through all the region of the Jordan

---

[170] 3:2-3

to prepare the way of the Lord,

to herald the coming of Jesus.

Glory to you, O Christ, Son of God!

To the waters of the Jordan you came

to be baptized by the hand of John.

Upon you the Spirit descended as a dove.

Above you the heavens opened,

and the voice of the Father was heard:

"This is my Son, the Beloved!"

From the river blessed by your presence

you went forth to baptize not only with water

but with fire and the Holy Spirit.

Glory to you, O Holy Spirit, Lord and Giver of life!

By your power, the Church is baptized,

going down with Christ into death

and rising with him to new life.

By your power, we are set free from sin

to become the children of God,

the glorious Body of Christ.

By your power, all fear is vanquished,

and the Gospel of love is preached

in every corner of the earth,

to the glory of God,

the Father, the Son and the Holy Spirit,

to whom be all praise in this Jubilee year

and in every age to come. Amen.

Chapter 2:
The Wedding at Cana

Saint John Paul II gave the following address on Wednesday, February 26, 1997 during his General Audience:

Jesus works miracle at Mary's request

In the episode of the wedding at Cana, St John presents Mary's first intervention in the public life of Jesus and highlights her co-operation in her Son's mission.

At the beginning of the account the Evangelist tells us that "the Mother of Jesus was there,"[171] and, as if to suggest that her presence was the reason for the couple's invitation to Jesus and his disciples,[172] he adds "Jesus also was invited to the marriage, with his disciples."[173] With these remarks, John seems to indicate that at Cana, as in the fundamental event of the Incarnation, it is Mary who introduces the Savior.

The meaning and role of the Blessed Virgin's presence become evident when the wine runs out. As a skilled and wise housewife, she immediately notices and intervenes so that no one's joy is marred and, above all, to help the newly married couple in difficulty.

---

[171] John 2:1
[172] cf. *Redemptoris Mater*, n. 21
[173] John 2:2

Turning to Jesus with the words: "they have no wine,"[174] Mary expresses her concern to him about this situation, expecting him to solve it. More precisely, according to some exegetes, his Mother is expecting an extraordinary sign, since Jesus had no wine at his disposal.

The choice made by Mary, who could perhaps have obtained the necessary wine elsewhere, shows the courage of her faith, since until that moment Jesus had worked no miracles, either in Nazareth or in his public life.

At Cana, the Blessed Virgin once again showed her total availability to God. At the Annunciation she had contributed to the miracle of the virginal conception by believing in Jesus before seeing him; here, her trust in Jesus' as yet unrevealed power causes him to perform his "first sign", the miraculous transformation of water into wine.

In that way she precedes in faith the disciples who, as John says, would believe after the miracle: Jesus "manifested his glory; and his disciples believed in him."[175] Thus, Mary strengthened their faith by obtaining this miraculous sign.

Jesus' answer to Mary's words, "O woman, what have you to do with me? My hour has not yet come,"[176] appears to express a refusal, as if putting his Mother's faith to the test.

---

[174] John 2:3
[175] John 2:11
[176] John 2:4

According to one interpretation, from the moment his mission begins Jesus seems to call into question the natural relationship of son to which his mother refers. The sentence, in the local parlance, is meant to stress a distance between the persons, by excluding a communion of life. This distance does not preclude respect and esteem; the term "woman" by which he addresses his Mother is used with a nuance that will recur in the conversations with the Canaanite woman,[177] the Samaritan woman,[178] the adulteress,[179] and Mary Magdalene,[180] in contexts that show Jesus' positive relationship with his female interlocutors.

With the expression: "O woman, what have you to do with me?", Jesus intends to put Mary's co-operation on the level of salvation which, by involving her faith and hope, requires her to go beyond her natural role of mother.

Of much greater import is the reason Jesus gives: "My hour has not yet come."[181]

Some scholars who have studied this sacred text, following St Augustine's interpretation, identify this "hour" with the Passion event. For others, instead, it refers to the first miracle in which the prophet of Nazareth's messianic power would be revealed. Yet others hold that the sentence is interrogative and an extension of the question that precedes it: "What have you to do with me? Has my

---

[177] cf. Matthew 15:28
[178] cf. John 4:21
[179] cf. John 8:10
[180] cf. John 20:13
[181] John 2:4

hour not yet come?" Jesus gives Mary to understand that henceforth he no longer depends on her, but must take the initiative for doing his Father's work. Then Mary docilely refrains from insisting with him and instead turns to the servants, telling them to obey him.

In any case her trust in her Son is rewarded. Jesus, whom she has left totally free to act, works the miracle, recognizing his Mother's courage and docility: "Jesus said to them, 'Fill the jars with water'. And they filled them up to the brim."[182] Thus their obedience also helps to procure wine in abundance.

Mary's request: "Do whatever he tells you", keeps its ever timely value for Christians of every age and is destined to renew its marvelous effect in everyone's life. It is an exhortation to trust without hesitation, especially when one does not understand the meaning or benefit of what Christ asks.

As in the account of the Canaanite woman,[183] Jesus' apparent refusal exalts the woman's faith, so that her Son's words, "My hour has not yet come", together with the working of the first miracle, demonstrate the Mother's great faith and the power of her prayer.

The episode of the wedding at Cana urges us to be courageous in faith and to experience in our lives the truth of the Gospel words: "Ask, and it will be given you."[184]

---

[182] John 2:7
[183] Matthew 15:24-26
[184] Matthew 7:7; Luke 11:9

Chapter 3:
The Proclamation of the Kingdom of Heaven

Saint John Paul II gave the following homily on the Feast of Christ the King, Sunday, November 23, 1997:

Jesus indicates his true kingship: "I am a king. For this I was born, and for this I have come into the world, to bear witness to the truth. Everyone who is of the truth hears my voice."[185]

He is not a king as the representatives of the Sanhedrin understood it: he does not, in fact, aspire to any political power in Israel. On the contrary, his kingdom goes well beyond the borders of Palestine. Everyone who is of the truth hears his voice and recognizes him as king.[186]

This is the universal scope of Christ's kingdom and its spiritual dimension.

"Bear witness to the truth."[187] The reading from the Book of Revelation says that Jesus Christ is "the faithful witness."[188] He is the faithful witness because he reveals the mystery of God and announc-

---

[185] John 18:37
[186] Ibid.
[187] Ibid.
[188] Revelation 1:5

es his kingdom, which is now present. He is the first Servant of this kingdom. By becoming "obedient unto death, even death on the cross,"[189] he will witness to the Father's power over creation and over the world. And the place for exercising his kingship is the Cross he embraces on Golgotha. His was a shameful death, but it represents a confirmation of the Gospel proclamation of the kingdom of God. In the eyes of his enemies, that death should have been proof that all he had said and done was false: "He is the King of Israel; let him come down now from the cross, and we will believe in him."[190] He did not come down from the cross but, like the Good Shepherd, he gave his life for his sheep.[191] The confirmation of his royal power, however, came a little later when on the third day he rose from the dead, revealing himself as "the first-born of the dead."[192]

He, the obedient Servant, is King because he has "the keys of death and Hades."[193] And, because he is the conqueror of death, hell and Satan, he is "the ruler of kings on earth."[194] In fact, everything on earth is subject to death. Instead, he who has power over death opens the prospect of immortal life to all humanity. He is the Alpha and the Omega, the beginning and the fulfillment of all creation,[195]

---

[189] Philippians 2:8
[190] Matthew 27:42
[191] cf. John 10:11
[192] Revelation 1:5
[193] Revelation 1:18
[194] Revelation 1:5
[195] cf. Revelation 1:8

so that every generation can repeat: Blessed is his kingdom that is coming.[196]

Dear brothers and sisters, [...] the truth about Christ the King is the fulfillment of the prophecies of the Old Testament. The prophet Daniel announces the coming of the Son of man, who has been given "dominion and glory and kingdom." He comes served by "peoples, nations and languages" and his "dominion is an everlasting dominion, which shall not pass away, and his kingdom one that shall not be destroyed."[197] We know well that all this was perfectly fulfilled in Christ, in his Passover of Death and Resurrection.

The Solemnity of Christ, King of the Universe, invites us to repeat with faith the prayer of the Our Father, which Jesus himself taught us: "Thy kingdom come."

Thy kingdom come, O Lord! — "A kingdom of truth and life, a kingdom of holiness and grace, a kingdom of justice, love and peace." Amen.

---

[196] cf. Mark 11:10
[197] cf. Daniel 7:14

Chapter 4:
The Transfiguration

Saint John Paul II gave the following homily on the Feast of the Transfiguration of the Lord and the 21st Anniversary of the death of Saint Pope Paul VI on Friday, August 6, 1999:

The Eucharist which we are preparing to celebrate takes us in spirit to Mount Tabor together with the Apostles Peter, James, and John, to admire in rapture the splendor of the transfigured Lord. In the event of the Transfiguration, we contemplate the mysterious encounter between history, which is being built every day, and the blessed inheritance that awaits us in heaven in full union with Christ, the Alpha and the Omega, the Beginning and the End.

We, pilgrims on earth, are granted to rejoice in the company of the transfigured Lord when we immerse ourselves in the things of above through prayer and the celebration of the divine mysteries. But, like the disciples, we too must descend from Tabor into daily life where human events challenge our faith. On the mountain we saw; on the paths of life we are asked tirelessly to proclaim the Gospel which illuminates the steps of believers.

This deep spiritual conviction guided the whole ecclesial mission of my venerable Predecessor, the [Saint] Paul VI, who returned to the Father's house precisely on the Feast of the Transfiguration,

21 years ago now. In the reflection he had planned to give at the Angelus on that day, 6 August 1978, he said: "The Transfiguration of the Lord, recalled by the liturgy of today's solemnity throws a dazzling light on our daily life, and makes us turn our mind to the immortal destiny which that fact foreshadows."

Yes! Paul VI reminds us: we are made for eternity and eternity begins at this very moment, since the Lord is among us and lives with and in his Church.

As we commemorate my unforgettable Predecessor in the see of Peter with deep emotion, let us pray that every Christian will know how to draw courage and constancy from contemplating Christ, who "reflects the glory of God and bears the very stamp of his nature,"[198] in order to proclaim and witness faithfully through his words and works.

May Mary, our tender and caring Mother, help us to be bright rays of the saving light of her Son Jesus.

---

[198] Hebrews 1:3

Chapter 5:
The Institution of the Eucharist

Saint John Paul II wrote the following as Chapter 6 of his encyclical Ecclesia de Eucharista *(On the Eucharist in its Relationship to the Church):*

At the School of Mary, "Woman of the Eucharist"

If we wish to rediscover in all its richness the profound relationship between the Church and the Eucharist, we cannot neglect Mary, Mother and model of the Church. In my Apostolic Letter *Rosarium Virginis Mariae,* I pointed to the Blessed Virgin Mary as our teacher in contemplating Christ's face, and among the mysteries of light I included the institution of the Eucharist.[199] Mary can guide us towards this most holy sacrament, because she herself has a profound relationship with it.

At first glance, the Gospel is silent on this subject. The account of the institution of the Eucharist on the night of Holy Thursday makes no mention of Mary. Yet we know that she was present among the Apostles who prayed "with one accord"[200] in the first community which gathered after the Ascension in expectation of

[199] cf. No. 21: AAS 95 (2003), 20.
[200] cf. Acts 1:14

Pentecost. Certainly Mary must have been present at the Eucharistic celebrations of the first generation of Christians, who were devoted to "the breaking of bread."[201]

But in addition to her sharing in the Eucharistic banquet, an indirect picture of Mary's relationship with the Eucharist can be had, beginning with her interior disposition. Mary is a "woman of the Eucharist" in her whole life. The Church, which looks to Mary as a model, is also called to imitate her in her relationship with this most holy mystery.

Mysterium fidei! If the Eucharist is a mystery of faith which so greatly transcends our understanding as to call for sheer abandonment to the word of God, then there can be no one like Mary to act as our support and guide in acquiring this disposition. In repeating what Christ did at the Last Supper in obedience to his command: "Do this in memory of me!", we also accept Mary's invitation to obey him without hesitation: "Do whatever he tells you."[202] With the same maternal concern which she showed at the wedding feast of Cana, Mary seems to say to us: "Do not waver; trust in the words of my Son. If he was able to change water into wine, he can also turn bread and wine into his body and blood, and through this mystery bestow on believers the living memorial of his Passover, thus becoming the "bread of life."

---

[201] Acts 2:42
[202] John 2:5

In a certain sense Mary lived her Eucharistic faith even before the institution of the Eucharist, by the very fact that she offered her virginal womb for the Incarnation of God's Word. The Eucharist, while commemorating the passion and resurrection, is also in continuity with the incarnation. At the Annunciation, Mary conceived the Son of God in the physical reality of his body and blood, thus anticipating within herself what to some degree happens sacramentally in every believer who receives, under the signs of bread and wine, the Lord's body and blood.

As a result, there is a profound analogy between the Fiat which Mary said in reply to the angel, and the Amen which every believer says when receiving the body of the Lord. Mary was asked to believe that the One whom she conceived "through the Holy Spirit" was "the Son of God."[203] In continuity with the Virgin's faith, in the Eucharistic mystery we are asked to believe that the same Jesus Christ, Son of God and Son of Mary, becomes present in his full humanity and divinity under the signs of bread and wine.

"Blessed is she who believed."[204] Mary also anticipated, in the mystery of the incarnation, the Church's Eucharistic faith. When, at the Visitation, she bore in her womb the Word made flesh, she became in some way a "tabernacle" – the first "tabernacle" in history – in which the Son of God, still invisible to our human gaze, allowed himself to be adored by Elizabeth, radiating his light as it were through the eyes and the voice of Mary. And is not the enraptured

---

[203] Luke 1:30-35
[204] Luke 1:45

gaze of Mary as she contemplated the face of the newborn Christ and cradled him in her arms that unparalleled model of love which should inspire us every time we receive Eucharistic communion?

Mary, throughout her life at Christ's side and not only on Calvary, made her own the sacrificial dimension of the Eucharist. When she brought the child Jesus to the Temple in Jerusalem "to present him to the Lord,"[205] she heard the aged Simeon announce that the child would be a "sign of contradiction" and that a sword would also pierce her own heart.[206] The tragedy of her Son's crucifixion was thus foretold, and in some sense Mary's *Stabat Mater* at the foot of the Cross was foreshadowed. In her daily preparation for Calvary, Mary experienced a kind of "anticipated Eucharist" – one might say a "spiritual communion" – of desire and of oblation, which would culminate in her union with her Son in his passion, and then find expression after Easter by her partaking in the Eucharist which the Apostles celebrated as the memorial of that passion.

What must Mary have felt as she heard from the mouth of Peter, John, James, and the other Apostles the words spoken at the Last Supper: "This is my body which is given for you"?[207] The body given up for us and made present under sacramental signs was the same body which she had conceived in her womb! For Mary, receiving the Eucharist must have somehow meant welcoming once more into her

---

[205] Luke 2:22
[206] cf. Luke 2:34-35
[207] Luke 22:19

womb that heart which had beat in unison with hers and reliving what she had experienced at the foot of the Cross.

"Do this in remembrance of me."[208] In the "memorial" of Calvary all that Christ accomplished by his passion and his death is present. Consequently all that Christ did with regard to his Mother for our sake is also present. To her he gave the beloved disciple and, in him, each of us: "Behold, your Son!" To each of us he also says: "Behold your mother!"[209]

Experiencing the memorial of Christ's death in the Eucharist also means continually receiving this gift. It means accepting – like John – the one who is given to us anew as our Mother. It also means taking on a commitment to be conformed to Christ, putting ourselves at the school of his Mother and allowing her to accompany us. Mary is present, with the Church and as the Mother of the Church, at each of our celebrations of the Eucharist. If the Church and the Eucharist are inseparably united, the same ought to be said of Mary and the Eucharist. This is one reason why, since ancient times, the commemoration of Mary has always been part of the Eucharistic celebrations of the Churches of East and West.

In the Eucharist the Church is completely united to Christ and his sacrifice, and makes her own the spirit of Mary. This truth can be understood more deeply by re-reading the *Magnificat* in a Eucharistic key. The Eucharist, like the Canticle of Mary, is first and foremost praise and thanksgiving. When Mary exclaims: "My soul magnifies

---

[208] Luke 22:19
[209] cf. John 19: 26-27

the Lord and my spirit rejoices in God my Savior," she already bears Jesus in her womb. She praises God "through" Jesus, but she also praises him "in" Jesus and "with" Jesus. This is itself the true "Eucharistic attitude".

At the same time, Mary recalls the wonders worked by God in salvation history in fulfillment of the promise once made to the fathers,[210] and proclaims the wonder that surpasses them all, the redemptive incarnation. Lastly, the *Magnificat* reflects the eschatological tension of the Eucharist. Every time the Son of God comes again to us in the "poverty" of the sacramental signs of bread and wine, the seeds of that new history wherein the mighty are "put down from their thrones" and "those of low degree are exalted,"[211] take root in the world. Mary sings of the "new heavens" and the "new earth" which find in the Eucharist their anticipation and in some sense their program and plan. The *Magnificat* expresses Mary's spirituality, and there is nothing greater than this spirituality for helping us to experience the mystery of the Eucharist. The Eucharist has been given to us so that our life, like that of Mary, may become completely a *Magnificat!*

---

[210] cf. Luke 1:55
[211] cf. Luke 1:52

About the Editor

Scott Smith is an author, attorney, and theologian from Louisiana. Scott is a lover of all things Catholic: the Eucharist, the Blessed Mother, and especially the King of Kings, Who is the hidden connection between all history, Scripture, culture, and theology.

Check out more of his writing and courses below ...

More from Scott Smith

Scott regularly contributes to his blog, The Scott Smith Blog at www.thescottsmithblog.com, WINNER of the 2018-2019 Fisher's Net Award for Best Catholic Blog:

FISHER'S NET AWARD
BEST CATHOLIC
BLOG 2018

— THE —
SCOTT SMITH BLOG
ALL ROADS LEAD TO ROME

AS SEEN ON ...
REGISTER
ChurchPOP
Aleteia
BIG PULPIT
New Advent
Catholic Online
SPIRIT DAILY
ALL SAINTS UNIVERSITY
CATHOLICISM.ORG

Scott's other books can be found at his publisher's, Holy Water Books, website, holywaterbooks.com, as well as on Amazon

His other books on theology and the Catholic faith include *The Catholic ManBook*, *Everything You Need to Know About Mary But Were Never Taught*, and *Blessed is He Who …* (Biographies of Blesseds). More on these below …

His fiction includes *The Seventh Word*, a pro-life horror novel, and the *Cajun Zombie Chronicles*, the Catholic version of the zombie apocalypse.

ALL SAINTS UNIVERSITY
EST. MMXVII

Scott has also produced courses on the Blessed Mother and Scripture for All Saints University.

Learn about the Blessed Mary from anywhere and learn to defend your mother! It includes over six hours of video plus a free copy of the next book ... Enroll Now!

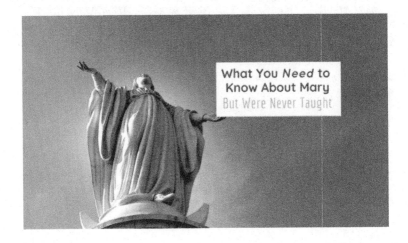

What You Need to Know About Mary But Were Never Taught

Give a robust defense of the Blessed Mother using Scripture. Now, more than ever, every Catholic needs to learn how to defend their mother, the Blessed Mother. Because now, more than ever, the family is under attack and needs its Mother.

Discover the love story, hidden within the whole of Scripture, of the Father for his daughter, the Holy Spirit for his spouse, and the Son for his MOTHER.

This collection of essays and the All Saints University course made to accompany it will demonstrate through Scripture how the Immaculate Conception of Mary was prophesied in Genesis.

It will also show how the Virgin Mary is the New Eve, the New Ark, and the New Queen of Israel.

Catholic Nerds Podcast

As you might have noticed, Scott is obviously well-credentialed as a nerd. Check out Scott's podcast: the Catholic Nerds Podcast on iTunes, Podbean, Google Play, and wherever good podcasts are found!

The Catholic ManBook

Do you want to reach Catholic Man LEVEL: EXPERT? *The Catholic ManBook* is your handbook to achieving Sainthood, manly Sainthood. Find the following resources inside, plus many others:

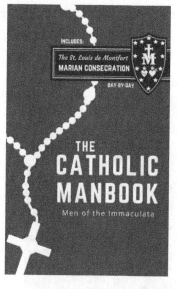

- Top Catholic Apps, Websites, and Blogs
- Everything you need to pray the Rosary
- The Most Effective Daily Prayers & Novenas, including the Emergency Novena
- Going to Confession and Eucharistic Adoration like a boss!
- Mastering the Catholic Liturgical Calendar

The Catholic ManBook contains the collective wisdom of The Men of the Immaculata, of saints, priests and laymen, fathers and sons, single and married. Holiness is at your fingertips. Get your copy today.

NEW! This year's edition also includes a revised and updated St. Louis de Montfort Marian consecration. Follow the prayers in a day-by-day format.

The Seventh Word

The FIRST Pro-Life Horror Novel!

Pro-Life hero, Abby Johnson, called it "legit scary ... I don't like reading this as night! ... It was good, it was so good ... it was terrifying, but good."

The First Word came with Cain, who killed the first child of man. The Third Word was Pharaoh's instruction to the midwives.

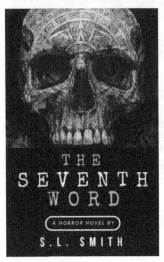

The Fifth Word was carried from Herod to Bethlehem. One of the Lost Words dwelt among the Aztecs and hungered after their children.

Evil hides behind starched white masks. The ancient Aztec demon now conducts his affairs in the sterile environment of corporate medical facilities. An insatiable hunger draws the demon to a sleepy Louisiana hamlet. There, it contracts the services of a young attorney, Jim David, whose unborn child is the ultimate object of the demon's designs. Monsignor, a mysterious priest of unknown age and origin, labors unseen to save the soul of a small town hidden deep within Louisiana's plantation country, nearly forgotten in a bend of the Mississippi River.

You'll be gripped from start to heart-stopping finish in this page-turning thriller from new author S.L. Smith.

With roots in Bram Stoker's Dracula, this horror novel reads like Stephen King's classic stories of towns being slowly devoured by an unseen evil and the people who unite against it.

The book is set in southern Louisiana, an area the author brings to life with compelling detail based on his local knowledge.

Blessed is He Who ...
Models of Catholic Manhood

You are the average of the five people you spend the most time with, so spend more time with the Saints! Here are several men that you need to get to know whatever your age or station in life. These short biographies will give you an insight into how to live better, however you're living.

From Kings to computer nerds, old married couples to single teenagers, these men gave us extraordinary examples of holiness:

- Pier Giorgio Frassati & Carlo Acutis – Here are two extraordinary **young men**, an athlete and a computer nerd, living on either side of the 20th Century
- Two men of royal stock, Francesco II and Archduke Eu-gen, lived lives of holiness despite all the world conspir-ing against them.
- There's also the **simple husband and father**, Blessed Luigi. Though he wasn't a king, he can help all of us treat the women in our lives as queens.

Blessed Is He Who ... Models of Catholic Manhood explores the lives of six men who found their greatness in Christ and His Bride, the Church. In six succinct chapters, the authors, noted historian Brian J. Costello and theologian and attorney Scott L. Smith, share with you the uncommon lives of exceptional men who will one day be numbered among the Saints of Heaven, men who can bring all of us closer to sainthood.

THANKS FOR READING! TOTUS TUUS

Made in the USA
Coppell, TX
22 December 2021

69911203R00080